War Of The Words

The Gulf War Quote By Quote

War Of The Words
The Gulf War Quote By Quote

Compiled And Edited By
Wes Janz & Vickie Abrahamson

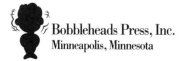
Bobbleheads Press, Inc.
Minneapolis, Minnesota

War Of The Words: The Gulf War Quote By Quote

© 1991 by Wes Janz and Vickie Abrahamson

Bobbleheads Press, Inc.
420 North Fifth Street, Suite 570
Minneapolis, Minnesota 55401 USA
(612) 338-1005

Printed in the United States of America
First Printing, September 1991

Library of Congress Catalog Card Number 91-75361
ISBN Number: 0-9630330-1-8

Book Design and Art Direction by Marcia Stone
Collages by Carl Wesley
Typesetting by Smart Set, Inc.

Factual material compiled in this publication was gathered through research of a number of sources, including the following:

Magazine Sources:
Adweek, Air Force Times, Asiaweek, The Atlantic, Aviation Week & Space Technology, The Bulletin of Atomic Scientists, Defense & Diplomacy, The Economist, Foreign Policy Bulletin, Harper's, India Today, Life, MacLean's, Mother Jones, The Nation, National Defense, National Geographic, The National Review, The New American, Newsweek, The New Yorker, People, People's Weekly World, Popular Mechanics, The Progressive, The Quayle Quarterly, Rolling Stone, Snowboard Industry News, Soldier of Fortune, Time, U.S. News & World Report, The Utne Reader

Newspaper Sources:
Atlanta Constitution, Boston Globe, Christian Science Monitor, Dallas Morning News, Detroit News, Funny Times, Los Angeles Times, Minneapolis StarTribune, Monticello Times, The New Statesman, The New Unionist, New York Amsterdam News, New York Times, New York Times Review of Books, USA Today, Village Voice, Wall Street Journal, Washington Post

Acknowledgments

For their help in the development of this book, we'd like to thank the designer
Marcia Stone; our research team headed by Brian Johnson and including
Will Niskanen, Kelly Nipper, Helen Greene, Robert Starzynski, Eric Whipperman
and Dean Janz; Pat Aafedt for her continuous advice; Jana Branch, Eric Malenfant
and Barry Engel for their design and production efforts, contributors Tom Stone
and Harry Kangis; the artist Carl Wesley, and Harvey Mackay for pushing us off the
dime with much, much more than a dime.

Contents

Preface

At 5:30 p.m. on January 16, 1991, I took my microwaved dinner and sat down to watch Peter Jennings and the ABC Nightly News. Like much of America, I had been waiting anxiously for an update on the escalating Persian Gulf Crisis. At 5:40, as if on cue, a correspondent dramatically cut in to report "flashes in the sky" over Baghdad. The Gulf War had begun and the world had prime-time, front row seats.

War Of The Words reports in the words of the participants the swirling, changing sands of this seven – month struggle. This was theater-in-the-round written and performed not only by George Bush, Saddam Hussein, and Norman Schwarzkopf, but by a cab driver in Algeria, a minister in California, a college exchange student in Spain, and a six-year-old British hostage.

This chronological quote book represents the viewpoints of these individuals and many others - world leaders and desert grunts, pro-war activists and anti-war demonstrators, conservative and liberal politicians; mothers, fathers, brothers, sisters, and friends; Christians, Jews, and Muslims; victors and the vanquished, friends and foes. All speak in words of equal importance.

There are several reasons why these divergent voices are worth remembering. First, the Gulf War was the initial post-Cold War conflict in which the Soviet Union and the United States shared the same basic viewpoints. This was a significant historical moment. It deserves an accurate chronological recounting that captures the entire script and its many twists and changing voices.

Second, this was an eye-opening clash of diverse cultural titans. This tragedy contains sub-plots of developed nations versus developing nations, of global agendas versus local disputes, and of contemporary values versus centuries-old beliefs. These sub-conflicts highlight the specific obstacles that any concept of "global village" or "one world community" must confront.

And third, the technology that brought the initial F-117A Stealth bombing runs into our homes "LIVE!" is the same technology that will ZAP! our attention spans to the next distraction, the next crisis. The newsprint and magazines that carried this war into our homes were probably discarded months ago. This time capsule, we hope, will enable the reader to accurately remember the world's varied responses to the accelerating crisis, and the lessons offered by the war.

Hopefully in the words and actions of the many participants, we can find insights into our shared world and common future.

Wes Janz
Minneapolis, Minnesota
August 1991

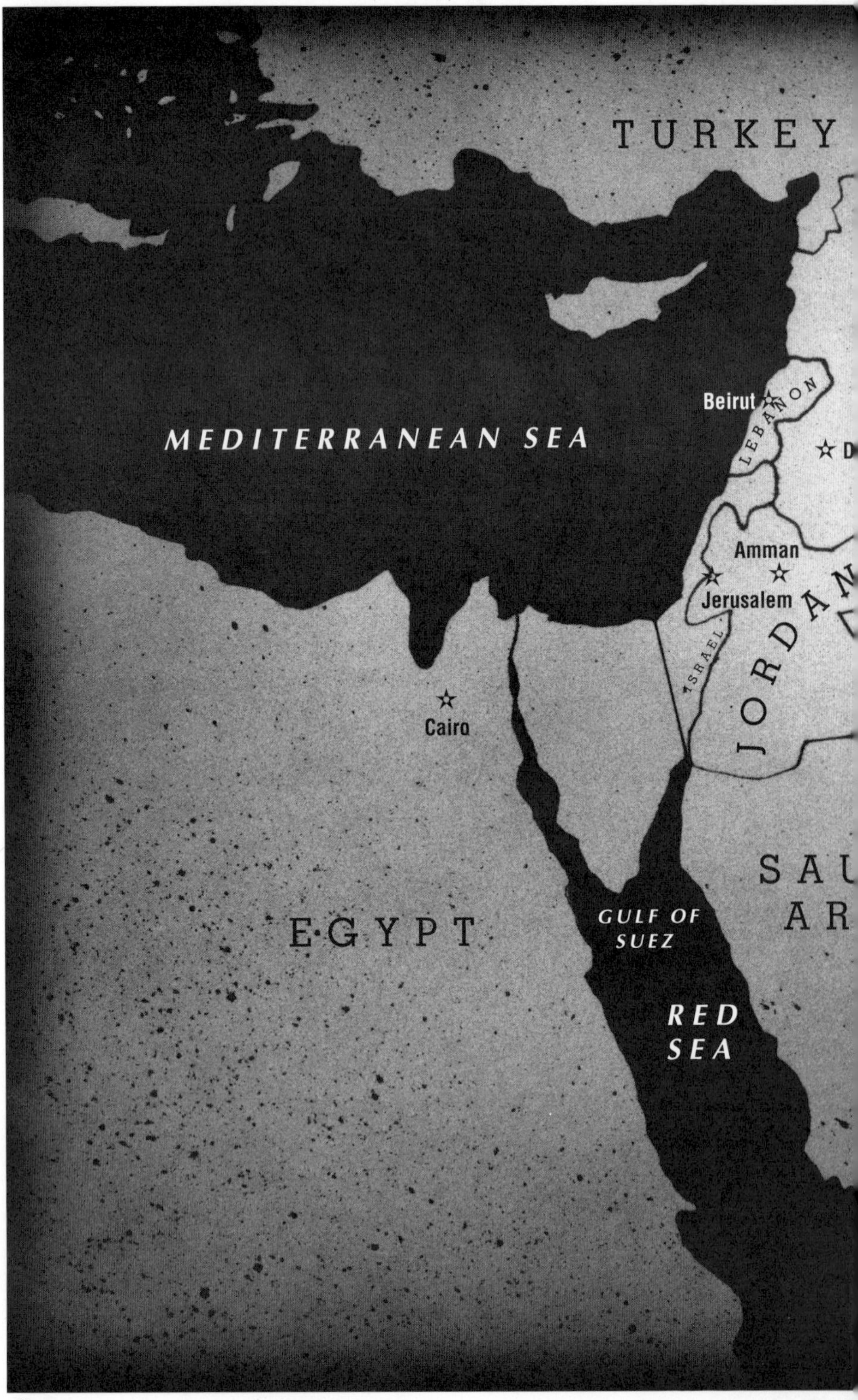
TURKEY
MEDITERRANEAN SEA
Beirut
LEBANON
Amman
Jerusalem
ISRAEL
JORDAN
Cairo
EGYPT
GULF OF
SUEZ
RED
SEA

SYRIA

IRAQ

☆
Baghdad

IRAN

☆
Tehran

Neutral
Zone

KUWAIT

☆ Kuwait
City

IA

Persian
Gulf

Dhahran ★

☆ Riyadh

War Of The Words

The Gulf War Quote By Quote

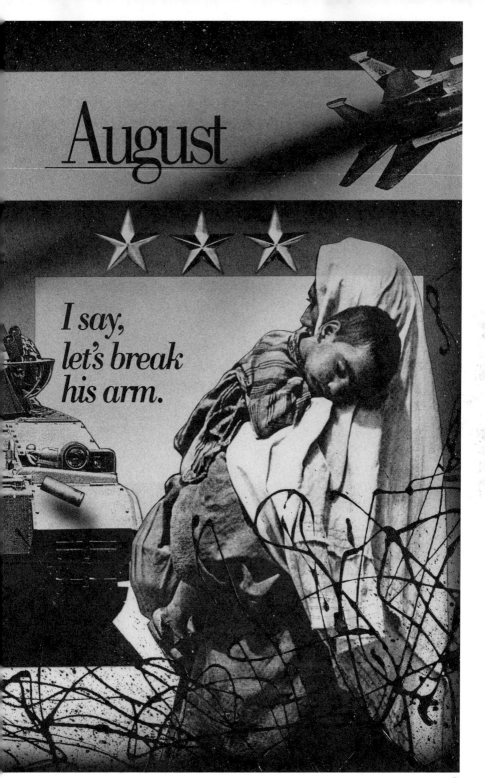

August 2

Greetings to the revolution in Kuwait.

Baghdad Radio

We're not ruling any options in, but we're not ruling any options out.

George Bush

President of the United States

Iraq army invades capital of Kuwait in fierce fighting

Headline

New York Times newspaper

Your country has been subjected to a barbaric invasion. It is your national duty to put up resistance by all possible means.

Kuwaiti Radio

I was lying in bed and I thought to myself, 'That is not a Kuwaiti Airlines jet taking off'... I had a bad feeling in my stomach, and I didn't get out of bed right away.

U.S. Army Chief Warrant Officer

recalling the opening assault on Kuwait City by Iraqi forces

Iraqi Troops Invade Kuwait

Bush Demands Iraqi Withdrawal And Calls For U.N. Emergency Session

They wanted to break (the Arab nation) into small parts and do something to ensure that the people aren't going to get back together... The West would do anything to prevent the rise of Islamic power.

Ryan LaHurd

Academic Dean of Augsburg College; Minneapolis, Minnesota on the division of the Arab world by Great Britain and France after World War I

It is a time of peace and diplomacy. Not for war and aggression. The world is watching what we do and will not be satisfied with vacillation and procrastination.

Thomas Pickering

U.S. envoy to the United Nations

It's all Kuwait's fault. They would be this adamant. They've brought this about.

King Fahd

of Saudi Arabia speaking to King Hussein of Jordan

FACT:

Saddam in Arabic means 'one who confronts.'

Q:

Time between the Kuwaiti Royal Family's limousine escape from their Dasman Palace residence and the taking of the residence by Iraqi troops, in minutes

A:

6

August 3

Saddam stuck his finger in our eye. I say, let's break his arm.

Representative William S. Broomfield

R-Michigan

There is no place for this sort of naked aggression in today's world.

President Bush

We swear … that we will make a graveyard for all those who think of committing aggression, starting with these cowardly American navies.

Baghdad Radio

referring to the embargo of Iraq

✝

[Hussein] must know that his insistence on the occupation of Kuwait and the threat against Saudi Arabia is an extreme act of provocation that would be met with force.

Reverend Jesse Jackson

Iraq will begin to withdraw its troops from Kuwait by Sunday.

Baghdad Radio

Iraq wants to show that it dominates the Middle East, that everyone has to line up behind it or else.

Barry Rubin

Senior fellow at the Washington Institute for Near East Policy

U.N. Demands Iraqi Withdrawal

Bush Embargos Iraqi Trade And Freezes Iraq's U.S. Assets

I don't think we have a military option at this moment, nor do we have a treaty obligation. I believe that our primary recourse should be very intensive diplomatic activity.

Senator Sam Nunn

D-Georgia, Chairman of the Senate Armed Forces Committee

I have been expecting a cross-border operation since Kuwait humiliated Iraq by refusing to write off debts. Saddam cannot tolerate this.

Mohammed Saadun

College graduate recently discharged from military service

*F*irst I think there's something positive in this matter. Hussein attacked an Arab state, so he won't attack us. It's too bad about Kuwait. But it's a fact.

Ezer Weisman

Former Israeli Defense Minister

*I*raqis will not forget the saying that cutting necks is better than cutting means of living. O God almighty, be witness that we have warned them!

Saddam Hussein

President of Iraq

Q:

Number of troops in Kuwait's pre-war standing army

A:

20,000

August 4-5

I have loved that man since I first heard about him.

Algerian taxi driver

referring to
Saddam Hussein

Rush, rush to our help.

Kuwaiti radio station's last message

We know they would like us to go beat up Iraq – then they can come out and condemn us and then go home and thank Allah 80 million times for what we did.

U.S. Administration official

on Saudi psychology

We can already detect a strong impulse on the part of many Arabs to think that they can put Saddam back in his cage by tossing him Kuwait as a bone.

Senior Bush administration official

Dear Marines: I'm very grateful that you and all the other people are willing to fight for our interests ...

Kimberly Osoria

Houston, Texas 6th grader

Just wait. Watch and learn.

President Bush

A joke told in Amman, Jordan:

Saddam Hussein was discussing with his chief of staff plans to outmaneuver the Americans. "How long did it take your men to capture Kuwait?"

The chief of staff replied, "Six hours, sir."

(continued)

The president asked, "If we were to take Saudi Arabia?"

"Twelve hours, sir."

"And the United Arab Emirates?"

"Another three hours' drive, sir."

"What about Bahrain?"

"We can take it by fax, sir."

There is absolutely no reason consumers should already be paying more for oil and gas. It's either panic or profiteering. Either way it must be stopped.

Senator Joseph Lieberman

D-Connecticut

FACT:

The area of Kuwait is 6,880 square miles, comparable in size to New Jersey. The area of Iraq is 167,925 square miles, comparable in size to California. Iraq is approximately 25 times the size of Kuwait.

Q:

Number of Iraqi troops in and around Kuwait City five hours after the invasion began

A:

100,000

August 6-12

A line has
been drawn
in the sand.

President Bush

All the Arabs
in the gulf
want us to
help them
against Iraq
even if they
can't say so.

Barry Rubin

*Senior fellow at the
Washington Institute for
Near East Policy*

"The only
thing I want
to know,"
Fahd said,
"is whether,
at the end of
this, Saddam
Hussein will
be able to
pick himself
up off the
floor."

Cheney said,
"No."

"We accept,"
said the king.

*King Fahd of
Saudi Arabia and
Richard Cheney,
United States
Secretary of
Defense*

*on U.S. troop deployment
to Saudi Arabia*

Me and
my brother
against my
cousin;
me, my
brother and
my cousin
against the
outsider.

Arab Proverb

The storm is
mighty. The
boat is small
and the oars
are short.

*White House
official*

on President Bush's position

Does George
Bush have
the right to
get us into a
third world
war from the
telephone on
his golf cart?

*Women Against
Military Madness*

This will
not stand.
This will not
stand, this
aggression
against
Kuwait.

President Bush

Iraq Announces Annexation Of Kuwait
Foreigners In Iraq And Kuwait Detained
Operation Desert Shield Begins

'What's the hottest movie in Kuwait this summer? Iraqnaphobia.'

Washington, D.C. joke

Kuwait is a country whose only territory is in hotel rooms in Saudi Arabia.

King Fahd

of Saudi Arabia

One of the fondest expressions around is that we can't be the world's policeman. But guess who gets called when suddenly someone needs a cop?

General Colin Powell

Chairman of the Joint Chiefs of Staff

If every country were to impose its illegitimate viewpoints through aggression and the use of force, the world would resemble a jungle.

Hafez al-Assad

President of Syria

Daddy is going over and kick butt.

Melissa DeForest

10-year-old daughter of Staff Sergeant Gene DeForest

Q:

Percentage of the world's crude oil reserves Iraq would control as a result of its annexation of Kuwait

A:

20%

August 13-18

I cannot remember a time when we had the world so strongly together against an action as now.

Margaret Thatcher

Prime Minister of Great Britain

If we had the technology back then, you would have seen Eva Braun on the "Donahue" show and Hitler on "Meet the Press."

Ed Turner

CNN Vice President defending the network's live coverage of Saddam Hussein

The people of Iraq have decided to play host to the citizens of these aggressive nations as long as Iraq remains threatened with an aggressive war.

Saadi Mahdi Saleh

Speaker of the Iraqi Parliament

I did not come away from that conversation with a feeling of hope.

President Bush

after meeting with King Hussein of Jordan

We would rather die than be humiliated. We will pluck out the eyes of those who attack the Arab nation.

Saddam Hussein

Iraq Peace Overture To Iran

Bush And King Hussein Meet; No Progress

Iraq Detains Foreigners

If Saddam moves, it is imperative to put that army, that regime, out of operation. And we would do it.

James Schlesinger

Former U.S. Secretary of Defense

I believe he is a person to be trusted and dealt with.

King Hussein

of Jordan, on Saddam Hussein

I told him that I may have to play G.I. Joe for awhile, and my son asked why, and I explained that you've got good G.I. Joes and bad G.I. Joes. You can't really get into politics with a 7-year-old.

Sergeant Michael Bruce

105th Military Airlift Group of the National Guard

Look out of your windows for birds dropping from the trees; cats, dogs and people dropping and choking; cars crashing; and general panic; which are signs of a gas attack.

Saudi pamphlet

Nobody can stand up forever to total economic deprivation.

President Bush

Q:

Bottles of suntan lotion the U.S. Army purchased in August from a K-Mart in Hinesville, Georgia

A:

25,500

August 19-24

*A*re you getting your milk, Stewart? And with corn flakes, too. I don't think all Iraqi kids can get corn flakes.

Saddam Hussein

speaking with 6-year-old British hostage

If hostages are used as human shields, the allies will hold war-criminal trials, and the goon we saw yesterday caressing that little boy's head will dangle from the gallows …

William Safire

New York Times newspaper

*T*here's nothing like contemplating the death of your son to make you focus your priorities …
If, as I expect, you eventually order American soldiers to attack Iraq, then it is God who will have to forgive you. I will not.

Alex Molnar

Father of a Marine, in a letter to President Bush

[*I*f the United States attacks] there will be columns of dead bodies which may have a beginning but will have no end.

Saddam Hussein

I told them I'd be back when I get back.

Jim Davenport

Pilot, U.S. Air Force Reserve 756th Military Airlift Squadron

Bush Calls Detained Foreigners 'Hostages'

Hussein Visits, Jokes With Hostages

U.N. Backs Economic Embargo Of Iraq

I would not risk a single life to restore the Kuwaiti royal family to the throne.

*Senator
Terry Sanford*

D-North Carolina

I don't see the point of intervening because the emir may be a nicer thug than Saddam Hussein.

Charles Oliver

Assistant editor of
Reason magazine

We are on the brink of catastrophe, unnecessarily. Without any reason American lives are being risked. For no reason whatsoever.

*Mohammed
Sadiq al-Mashat*

Iraq's ambassador to
the United States

FACT:

*The first F-117A
Nighthawk stealth
fighters left Tonopah
Test Range, Nevada,
for the Mideast on
August 19.*

Q:

*Number of times
F-15C Eagle fighter
planes would refuel
on their 6,500 mile,
14-hour flight from
the eastern U.S. to
Saudi Arabia*

A:

7

It's like two kids saying to one another, 'Knock that chip off my shoulder.'

*Robert
Kupperman*

Senior fellow at the Center
for Strategic and
International Studies,
on Bush and Hussein

It's probably worse in New York than it is over there.

*Reservist and
narcotics
detective*

from New York City

August 25-31

*A*ll the movies and television show Arabs as either terrorists, sheiks or belly dancers. We haven't seen one movie in which Arabs are depicted as real people. The message is always, 'Kill them.'

Osama Sablami

Publisher of
Sada al-Watan,
the largest Arabic-language
newspaper in the U.S.

If we remain firm and if we keep open the prospect that we will not stop, he will settle.

Henry Kissinger

Former U.S. Secretary of
State, on Saddam Hussein

*P*eople are talking about giving Saddam Hussein a face-saving solution. But whatever you do, don't save his face.

Amatzia Bar-Am

Professor at Haifa
University, Israel

He may end up being the first President who's held hostage on a cigarette boat. He's sort of got himself in a position where he has to go fishing even if he doesn't want to.

Jody Powell

Former Press Secretary

Iraq Tells Its Ships Not To Resist Embargo

Bush Dispatches Cabinet On International Multibillion Dollar Fundraising Tour

It's hot, but not any hotter than army gear and a helmet. Well, I'd rather be hot than – you know.

Elizeur Shurow

of Kibbutz Hazorea, whose factory makes chemical warfare suits

Get Their Gas And Kick-Their Ass

Banner

stretched across I-75 in northern Georgia

I would sit on my bed looking out the window down the Kennebunk River and I could almost see those destroyers on the horizon. At any moment I thought we were going to war.

One of the President's advisers

In a day he would be decimated. It would be over in a day.

Captain Jay Yakeley

Commander of the air wing on the U.S.S. Independence

FACT:

King Fahd and his court did not permit the Saudi press to report the Iraqi invasion of Kuwait until four days after it occurred.

Q:

Amount paid by a Kuwaiti citizen group to the public relations firm of Hill & Knowlton between August 20 and October 31 to publicize Kuwait's cause

A:

$5,640,000

Mideast Chronology

1534: The Ottoman Turks, ruling from Istanbul, conquer Baghdad

1917: The Ottomans relinquish control of Baghdad to Britain

1920: The British install Emir Faisal as King of Iraq

1932: The independent state of Iraq is formally admitted to the League of Nations

1933: King Faisal dies and is succeeded by his son Ghazi

1936: General Sidqi overthrows the Iraqi government

1937: Sidqi is assassinated by army officers
Six more coups follow in quick succession, ending in 1941
Saddam Hussein is born in a village near Takrit

1943: The Arab Ba'ath Movement, a group of ten people, publishes its first program in Damascus

1948-49: Israel declared an independent state

1958: The Iraqi monarchy of King Faisal II is toppled in a coup led by General Qassim

1959: Qassim survives an assassination attempt by a Ba'athist hit team, one of whose members is Saddam Hussein

1960: OPEC (Organization of Petroleum Exporting Countries) formed by Iraq, Kuwait, Iran, Saudi Arabia, and Venezuela

1961: Kuwait gains independence
British troops stop Iraqi attempt to annex Kuwait
Iraq army launches first major offensive against the Kurds

1963: A Ba'athist coup overthrows Qassim, and is itself toppled nine months later

1966: Saddam Hussein founds the Ba'athist party's secret police

1967: Israel defeats Egypt in Six-Day War

1968: Ba'athist Party seizes leadership of Iraq; Ahmad Hassan Al-Bakr becomes president; Saddam Hussein is second in command

1974: Kurdish autonomy accords collapse; full-scale fighting breaks out; hundreds of thousands of Kurds flee Iraq

1975: Iran ends support of the Kurds and Iraq gives up half of the Shatt al-Arab waterway in return

1978: Ayatollah Ruhollah Khomeini is expelled from Iraq

1979: Saddam Hussein becomes president of Iraq and promptly purges party elite
Ayatollah Khomeini establishes Islamic Republic in Iran
Egypt and Israel sign Camp David agreement
Soviet troops invade Afghanistan

1980: Iran-Iraq war begins

1981: Israel destroys Iraqi nuclear reactor

1982: U.S. Marines enter Lebanon

1983: U.S. Marine barracks bombed in Beirut, 241 killed
Turkey invades Iraqi Kurdistan with the full cooperation of the Iraqi regime

1984: U.S. Marines complete withdrawal from Lebanon

1986: U.S. bombs Libya

1987: An Iraqi fighter shoots at the U.S.S. Stark killing 37 of its crew
The U.S. reflags Kuwaiti oil tankers

1988: Kurds are gassed by Iraqi Army in first-ever use of chemical weapons by a state against its own citizens
The U.S.S. Vincennes shoots down an Iranian airbus, killing all 290 passengers
Iran-Iraq war ends

1989: Iraq and Saudi Arabia sign a non-aggression pact

1990: Iraq accuses Kuwait of stealing oil from Iraqi part of Rumailah oil field
Iraq invades Kuwait and declares its formal annexation as Iraq's nineteenth province

1991: Multinational forces led by the U.S. drive Iraq from Kuwait

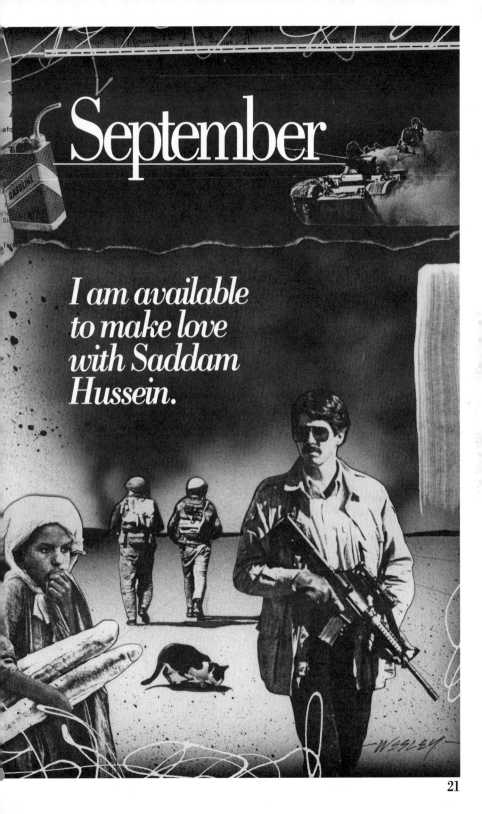

September

I am available to make love with Saddam Hussein.

September 1-4

We do not have an energy policy. We like to waste on the one hand and exploit on the other.

Henry Feninger

President of Get Oil Out

We have a war-tested society and a war-tested economy. So even if we have to eat mud, we can resist the pressure and not kneel down to any power.

Naji al-Hadithi

Director General of Iraq's Information Ministry

There is not going to be any war unless the Iraqis attack.

General H. Norman Schwarzkopf

Commander of U.S. forces in the Middle East

I wasn't a guest; I damn near starved to death.

Lloyd Culbertson

Released hostage

You invaded Panama, you invaded Grenada. So we invaded Kuwait.

Two Iraqi soldiers to an American lawyer

Any sign of Israeli weakness, whether real or perceived, cannot but whet the appetite of the Saddams of this world.

Jerusalem Post newspaper

Some Women And Children Hostages Leave Baghdad

U.S. Jets Deployed In 5 Mideast Countries

The United States can't be an arbiter of Arab differences and at the same time the strategic ally of their enemy Israel.

Hussein A. Hammami

Jordan's ambassador to the United States

I call it hell.

Captain John C. Ross

on his desert base in Saudi Arabia

When Mr. Hussein invaded Kuwait, one of the first things he did was change the name of the main hospital there from Al-Sabah Hospital to the Saddam Hussein Hospital. He has an affection for buildings named after himself.

Thomas L. Friedman

New York Times newspaper

Iraqi forces are not ten feet tall; they're about four feet tall. But remember, two four-footers can still take down a six-foot man.

Anthony Cordesman

Military strategist

The present situation is very explosive.

Javier Perez de Cuellar

Secretary General of the United Nations

Q:

Time between landings of U.S. airplanes in Saudi Arabia during Operation Desert Shield, in minutes

A:

7

September 5-8

I am available to make love with Saddam Hussein to achieve peace in the Middle East.

Ilona Staller

Italian Parliament member and former porn star

Sanctions are for the rich.

Ranjan Wijeratne

Sri Lanka's Deputy Defense Minister, defending his nation's refusal to cut off shipments of tea to Iraq

I lost my job, I lost my pension, I lost my savings, I lost my household, I lost everything. Before August 2, I was feeling myself to be rich. Now, I am feeling myself to be a beggar.

Duwood Ismail

Asian refugee from Kuwait

The standoff can't last forever. We build, Saddam Hussein builds, there's hyperactivity everywhere. I'd say that it comes to a head in six months, maximum, maybe a whole lot sooner.

Representative Les Aspin

D-Wisconsin, Chairman of the House Armed Services Committee

Stand firm, be patient and remain united so that together we can show that aggression does not pay.

President Bush

When that Iraq news comes on, I switch, unless it's interrupting a soap opera.

Mildred Birdsong

of Ohio

U.S. Forgives Egypt's $7 Billion Debt

Kuwait Pledges $2.5 Billion To Military Campaign

Playing the cynical game with dictators may be a necessity at times. Playing the patsy isn't.

Stephen Budiansky

U.S. News and World Report magazine

I'd throw the H-bomb at them.

Jerome Cumminsky

79-year-old former insurance salesman

The President loves the game 'Bet you can't keep up with us', and, since television is crisis-oriented, we love the game of 'Oh, yes we can.'

Susan Zirinsky

CBS producer

The Iraqi invasion of Kuwait is one of the defining moments of a new era ... we must seize this opportunity to solidify the ground rules of the new order.

James A. Baker

United States Secretary of State

A lot of people are worried the blacks are going to take over, and sending them is some slick way of thinning them out.

Eugene Patrick

A black mechanic

Q:

Pounds of weightlifting gear shipped by Arnold Schwarzenegger to U.S. troops in Saudi Arabia

A:

40,000

September 9-12

We didn't dare answer the phone, or answer the door, or leave the lights on at night.

Kristine Knutson

American held in Kuwait as Iraq's 'guest'

Iraq will not be permitted to annex Kuwait. And that's not a threat, not a boast. It's just the way it's going to be.

President Bush

The West cannot really afford to let Saddam Hussein go smiling home with two islands and an oil field in his pocket.

Douglas Hurd

British Foreign Secretary

You feel like you are in a parade when you walk down the street because so many people are always waving at you.

Airman First Class Bryan Westly

on the Saudi people

Bush And Gorbachev Meet In Helsinki

Iraq Offers Free Oil To Third World

Bush Addresses Congress

No peaceful international order is possible if larger states can devour their smaller neighbors.

President Bush and President Gorbachev

Joint Statement at the Helsinki Summit

No surrender even if we starve to death. The economic blockade will fail, and Iraq will triumph.

Protest sign in Baghdad

We will not stoop to the level of using human beings as bargaining chips ever.

Margaret Thatcher

Prime Minister of Great Britain

FACT:

In 1979 two Middle East leaders came to power: the Ayatollah Khomeini on February 1 and Saddam Hussein on July 16. On September 22, the eight-year war between Iran and Iraq began.

Q:

Number of Iraqis killed and wounded, respectively, in the eight-year Iran-Iraq War

A:

120,000 and 300,000

September 13-16

For God's sake, before we strangle here, tell your people to take your armies back. Go home and leave us alone!

Bassam E. Kakish

Retired general speaking of the embargo's effect on Aqaba, Jordan's only port

---

I don't know what to do. I have 18 years of research notes and materials on archaeology of the Gulf states, four huge case files over there, and I can't get at them.

Dr. Theresa Howard-Carter

No Christmas trees this year. We're going to be here a long time.

Colonel Walt Mather

in Saudi Arabia

Who's still here? There are no men older than 18 and younger than 40.

Linda James

at Twentynine Palms, California, the nation's largest Marine base

---

When Iraq returns to the path of peace, when Iraqi troops withdraw from Kuwait, when that country's rightful government is restored, when all foreigners held against their will are released, then, and then alone, will the world end the sanctions.

President Bush

I don't read about that stuff. I read about convicted killers being released, because I want to know where they are.

Sherri Baker

Boston housewife

*E*very piece of mail is like gold out here.

Sergeant William Darnell

We ate a lot of tuna fish, but there was food. We were washing our clothes in the embassy swimming pool, but we had enough water so that we weren't drinking from the pool.

Eleanor Mireles

on conditions at the U.S. embassy in Kuwait

For those who believe that superpower detente equals global peace, the invasion should provide an early corrective.

Straits Times newspaper

We're the biggest deadbeats in paying our dues to the United Nations.

Secretary of State James Baker

Q:

Amount that the United Nations claims it is owed by the United States government

A:

$718,000,000

September 17-20

The cutting edge would be in downtown Baghdad. If I want to hurt you, it would be at home, not out in the woods someplace.

General Michael J. Dugan

Air Force Chief of Staff

To speculate about what may or may not be included in a plan that might or might not be implemented is inappropriate.

Secretary of Defense Richard Cheney

after dismissing General Dugan

Saddam Hussein tells you that this crisis is a struggle between Iraq and America. In fact, it is Iraq against the world.

President Bush

in televised message to the Iraqi people

Four days ago I watched the Iraqis execute the manager of the Ardia supermarket because he refused to hang a picture of Saddam Hussein on the wall.

Havrad Ibrahim Shaya

Retired Kuwaiti Army Colonel

General Dugan Fired

Iraq Freezes Foreign Assets Of Countries Upholding Sanctions

Dan Rather, Sam Donaldson, Tom Brokaw, Ted Koppel, Forrest Sawyer, Garrick Utley, and Harry Smith went to Baghdad. Saddam Hussein let them all go free – an act of glowering malice that shall not be forgiven for seventy times seven years.

National Review magazine

One of the most spectacular end-runs around the Constitution ... I have ever witnessed.

Representative David Obey

D-Wisconsin, on U.S. Secretary of Defense Richard Cheney's seeking permission to use foreign money donated to the U.S. military buildup without prior Congressional approval

They tore down everything and carted away my life's possessions. They rubbed excrement on the walls and left nothing except the floorboards.

Kuwaiti businessman

The U.S. should know perfectly well that Iraq is not the tiny island of Grenada.

Baghdad Observer newspaper

Q:

Amount of monthly hazardous duty pay ordered by U.S. Secretary of Defense Richard Cheney for each of 150,000 U.S. troops in the Persian Gulf

A:

$110

September 21-24

Fill Stomachs, Not Body Bags

Seattle peace activist saying

No Slack For Iraq

Saying on a T-shirt

We will never allow anybody, whoever he may be, to strangle the people of Iraq without having himself strangled.

Iraqi leaders

on the embargo

Uncle George WANTS YOU to forget Failing Banks, Education, Drugs, AIDS, Poor Health Care, Unemployment, Crime, Racism, Corruption ... And Have a GOOD WAR

Free poster

offered by Village Voice newspaper

The meek shall inherit the earth. But for goodness' sake, just how meek must they be?

Crown Prince Hassan

of Jordan

Nobody could stay awake through that.

President Bush

on Saddam Hussein's proposal to send a 90-minute tape for U.S. viewing

World Bank Predicts $65 A Barrel Oil If War Breaks Out In Middle East

Final Flight Of American Women And Children Leaves Iraq

He clearly models his strategy after [James] Bond's old enemy Spectre ... Bond villains loved to say, 'No, no, Meester Bond, you are not a prisoner. Shall we call you our ... guest.'

Alexander Cockburn

The Nation magazine

*T*his man, I think he wants to be in show business, not politics. Every time he is on television he is dressed up differently, sometimes a king, sometimes a Bedouin. Next he will be a cowboy.

Nabila Naki

Egyptian woman, on Saddam Hussein

A circus buffoon who is dancing on American ropes ... vomiting poison like a spotted serpent.

The Iraqi Press

speaking of British Prime Minister Margaret Thatcher

We kissed Arafat on the cheek for years in the name of Arab brotherhood. No more. He's a thug.

Saudi official

Q:

Estimated number of princes in Saudi Arabia

A:

6,500

September 25-30

*F*or Bush it's like looking at El Greco's painting of Toledo; the sky is black and you know there's a tremendous storm coming, but for now there's an eerie calm.

Stephen Wayne

Presidential scholar, Georgetown University

America poses a threat to mankind.

Saddam Hussein

Saddam managed to market himself as the Robin Hood who was going to redistribute Arab wealth.

Assad Abdul Rahman

Palestine Liberation Organization analyst

*F*rom The Same Asylum That Brought You Khaddafy Duck ... Middle East Looney Tunes Presents: Yosemite Saddam!!!

G.I. T-shirt

in Saudi Arabia

The days of Hitler will not return .... It seems that Saddam Hussein reads only the first few pages of his history books and is unaware of the fate in store for tyrants who violate the independence of nations.

Al-Akhbar newspaper Cairo, Egypt

U.N. Votes To Impose Air Embargo

Bush Sells 5 Million Barrels Of Oil From U.S. Strategic Petroleum Reserve

Worldwide gasoline rationing could be among the first direct results of a full-scale conflict. Further along ... the casualties could involve the financial collapse of developing countries, outright failure of the economic reforms in Eastern Europe and a severe

(continued)

shock to the world banking system.

Christopher Flavin

Worldwatch Institute

The Council simply gave the green light to the United States and others to do what they were already doing.

Ricard Alarcon de Quesada

Cuba's delegate to the United Nations

If the President of the United States felt it was necessary for us to be here, that's 100 percent enough for me.

Army Sergeant Sinclair Thorne

Chemicals, chemicals, O Saddam!

Jordanian Muslim militants at a rally

Q:

Number of times Saddam Hussein repeated to Diane Sawyer of ABC-TV news that he "was not Ceausescu" in reference to the repressive, one-party leader of Romania who was killed after his overthrow

A:

3

A G.I. Family's Prayer

Hear, Lord, my prayer for my G.I.,
so eager to live – too young to die.

Beneath an alien blistering sun,
he faces a dangerous enemy gun.

The storm clouds gather, the horror of war,
my soldier stands bravely guarding the door.

Defending justice, peace, and freedom,
to his Commander-in-Chief give Holy wisdom.

From war's alarms, bring swift release.
Hasten the day of honorable peace.

On land and sand and sea and air,
I back my soldier with this prayer:

"No matter how far he's forced to roam,
just bring, I pray, my G.I. home."

Amen

Robert H. Schuller

Reprinted by permission of Dr. Robert H. Schuller of the Crystal Cathedral Ministries

From A Distance

From a distance
You look like my friend
Even though we are at war.

From a distance
I can't comprehend
What all this war is for.

From a distance
There is harmony
And it echoes through the land
It's the hope of hope
It's the hope of love
It's the heart of every man.

Lyrics of Grammy-winning song by Julie Gold

BRING THE TROOPS' HOME NOW!

PEACE

October

No blood for oil.

October 1-7

We must rid ourselves of Saddam Hussein before he achieves the means to rid himself of us.

William Safire

New York Times
newspaper

Dwarfs led by Bush and his two servants Fahd and Hosni ...

*Iraq's
Revolutionary
Command
Council*

describing leaders of the
Allied coalition

The U.S. has extended two helping hands, while other nations have lent their pinkie fingers.

Rizvan A. Mirza

Ankara, Turkey

In war, the first casualty is truth.

*The Montana
Green Party*

When the doors for peace are closed, the ghosts of war will start appearing.

*Prince Sultan
bin Abdulaziz*

Saudi defense minister

... and another country invaded it [Kuwait] and we cannot have that.

*First Lady
Barbara Bush*

explaining the crisis to
her grandchildren

Bush Addresses U.N.

Congress Endorses Bush's Gulf Policy

Hussein Visits Troops In Kuwait

It takes a special person to serve our country.

New Hallmark card for the Gulf Crisis

We could nuke Baghdad into glass, wipe it with Windex, tie fatback on our feet and go skating.

Fred Reed

Air Force columnist, on American nuclear possibilities

In a war, the American soldiers are a new kind of foreign worker here. We have Pakistanis driving taxis and now we have Americans defending us.

Teacher

in Saudi Arabia

I say to the representative of the Iraqi regime, we are going back, God willing – we are going back to Kuwait.

Dhara Razzooqi

Kuwait Foreign Ministry Director of International Organizations

FACT:

Per capita, Kuwait is the world's richest nation.

Q:

World rank of the Soviet Union and the United States in dollar amount of arms sold in 1989

A:

1, 2

Soviet Union $11,700,000,000;

United States $10,800,000,000;

World Total $31,800,000,000

October 8-10

I don't want to wear it – I want to be a ninja.

Three-year-old Israeli boy

on his gas mask

*T*he mission of our troops is wholly defensive. They will not initiate hostilities but they will defend themselves ...

President Bush

*A*ll the fleets, planes in the world, whether inside or outside the Arab homeland, will not shake the palm fronds.

Statement of Iraq's ruling Revolutionary Command Council

*T*his is the ballgame. On a scale of 1 to 10, with 10 a total disaster, no Arab ground troops means a 9, and no ground troops from anyone but us and the Arabs means about a 12.

Representative Les Aspin

D-Wisconsin, Chairman of the House Armed Services Committee

*W*hen Iraq shucked off the traditional limits of Arab politics the Saudis decided to shuck off their Arab nationalist scruples too. They understood that this time they could not bury their heads in the sand and wait for the storm to blow over.

Fouad Ajami

Director of Middle East Studies at Johns Hopkins University

Israel Gives Gas Masks To Citizens

British, Australian And U.S. Ships Fire Warning Shots Across Iraqi Ship Bow

I hope we won't be the Lone Ranger the way we were in Vietnam.

Senator
Alan Cranston

D-California

For the first time since World War II, we are virtually acting as allies.

Maksim Yusin

Soviet journalist, on
U.S.-Soviet cooperation
in the Gulf

It's not the Gulf crisis but the stories of the gas masks that are worrying American tourists. Tourists are asking if they will also be given gas masks.

Offer Eshed

Manager of Ophiel Tours
in Tel Aviv

It would take a T.S. Lawrence to get those guys to act in concert. And I haven't noticed any Lawrences in the corridors of the Pentagon.

Analyst

on Saudi-American
cooperation

The boundary between the Saudi state treasury and the Saudi personal coffers is rather permeable.

Yahya Sadowski

Brookings Institute

Q:

Number of gas masks
issued in Israel

A:

4,600,000

October 11-15

*F*ellow Americans, I have sent our troops to the Middle East ... They are there to defend the security ... the value ... the principle we hold dear – 18 miles per gallon ...

Caption

from a Boston Globe newspaper cartoon

*U*ltimately the only way to escape from this dilemma is to escape from oil, which pollutes the sea, the land, the air, politics, the economy, and much else besides.

Bernard Lewis

Princeton University

*T*he task now is turning 'what ifs' into 'maybes' and 'maybes' into 'cans' and 'cans' into 'yes, doables' and 'doables' into 'agreeds.'

Yevgeny Primakov

Soviet emissary to Iraq

*H*e is a man without scruples, a killer and a murderer on a vast scale. This is pan-Arabism with a bayonet, chemical weapons and a whip for all those who will not submit.

Fouad Ajami

Director of Middle East Studies at Johns Hopkins University, on Saddam Hussein

U.N. Condemns Israel For Killing Palestinian Demonstrators In Jerusalem

Hussein Offers Withdrawal Proposal

Kuwait is the 19th province of Iraq, and this fact will not be changed whatsoever even if we have to fight a long war for that.

Latif Jassim

Iraq's Minister of Culture and Information

Why should we be involved? We could get oil from Mexico.

Katie Shafer

Miami

These are heavy-lift cargo ships. This is not for a one-night stand.

Pentagon official

on equipment sent to the Gulf

Saddam is coming! He's on his way! Saddam is going to sweep you away!

Shouts from Palestinian youths

Basically, our main interest in Saudi Arabia and Kuwait comes down to a three-letter word — oil. It is oil, oil and oil.

Representative Patricia Schroeder

D-Colorado

They ran out of deodorant but they are doing the best they can.

Margie Howett

wife of the American ambassador in Kuwait

Q:

Estimated minimum number of assassination attempts Saddam Hussein has survived in his 12 years as Iraq's president

A:

6

October 16-18

We are striking a blow for the principle that might does not make right.

President Bush

You hit a mine and that's it. You're through. It's one of the hazards of the job.

Sergeant Errol Thompson

Commander of a Bradley Fighting Vehicle

If President Saddam Hussein says something, the whole nation says the same. Where Kuwait is concerned, our motto is 'Victory or Death!'

Jafer al-Barazanji

Iraqi civilian official

Tell George Bush to get off the golf course and out of his fishing boat and come out here in the desert to take a look at what we're doing and drink some hot water with us.

Private Brett Thompson

There are a lot of overbuilt expectations. I think this is a nothing-burger.

White House Official

on King Hussein's peace mission

Shared responsibility for war is what the founding fathers intended.

Senator Claiborne Pell

D-Rhode Island

Bush Suggests Iraqi War-Crimes Trials
Baker Rejects Any 'Partial Solution'

Killing is very easy for them. It suffices to find a picture of the Emir in a home or, worse, a pamphlet for the person to be taken away, tortured, interrogated and then maybe executed.

Ismail al-Shatti

Professor at the College of Technological Studies in Kuwait after leaving Kuwait

The United States got three resolutions on Iraq out of the Security Council in five days, and it spent five days obstructing a Palestine resolution.

Jamil Halil

Director of the Palestine Liberation Organization's Information Office in Tunis

Iraq, Kuwait, Jordan, Syria, Saudi Arabia and so forth are hardly nations as we understand the term. They are quarrels with borders.

P.J. O'Rourke

Rolling Stone magazine

FACT:

WHHY-FM in Montgomery, Alabama held an "Insane Hussein" party. The first 102 cars received five free gallons of gasoline. A dunking booth featured a Saddam Hussein look-alike.

Q:

Average amount of gasoline President Bush's high performance boat Fidelity consumes per hour, in gallons

A:

25

October 19-21

No blood for oil.

Peace activist saying

What Iraq is doing to Kuwait is indecent and in Baghdad inhumane and absolutely outrageous.

Secretary of State James Baker

We like Saddam Hussein. He is courageous. He wants all Arabs to be equal. He wants to give the money of the rich Arabs to the poor Arabs. The emirs gave us nothing.

Tunisian policeman

Just because they've done so so far, you don't blithely assume that the Iraqis will respect diplomatic protocols forever. It's like a Baghdad version of musical chairs: You don't want to be here when the music stops.

Diplomat at the American Embassy

The principle preoccupation of these Saudi old-timers is to preserve prosperity. They do not want to risk it all because they know what it is like to have nothing, and they are proud of what they have built in this desert landscape.

Western diplomat

Oh, the good times are over. It was exciting to land all that equipment over there and watch the buildup ... we may soon face the hideous choice of pull out or go in, and George Bush has not really prepared the American public for this choice.

Senator Daniel Patrick Moynihan

D-New York

I look around, as they say from the Atlantic Ocean to the Gulf, and I see not a single Arab I would like to emulate. This is our time to assert an independent Saudi personality.

Motasim Hajaj

Saudi real estate executive

*T*he idea is that they die first so that no one can say Arabs did not participate in the war against Iraq, or that Saudis did not defend their country.

Marine commander

on Saudi forces stationed on the front lines

Any war here will leave in its wake such misery and huge losses, no matter how it goes. I don't think anything is worth that.

Ishaq al-Sehsah

Saudi doctor

Q:

Number of pre-Gulf War non-Kuwaitis living in Kuwait

A:

1,300,000 (two-thirds of the total population)

October 22-28

America is the head of the snake.

Jordanian saying

They can only hate one of us at a time. One week it was Saddam Hussein, one week it was Newt Gingrich, and me today.

Edward J. Rollins, Jr.

Co-chairman of the National Congressional Committee, shrugging off a White House attack

What Saddam Hussein says is logical and reasonable. The only problem is that it comes from him.

A Yemeni intellectual

There were no toilets. The food consisted of rice and tomato water, which we discovered we were supposed to use to help soften the stale bread we were fed.

Jim Thomson

Freed British hostage

Every time we 'send in the Marines' and other U.S. troops, we are sending proportionately more African-American and other youths of color, and more working-class white youth, than we are sending white middle- and upper-class youth.

Meiklejohn Civil Liberties Institute

Iraqi Freighter Halted And Boarded

Cheney Considers Additional Troops

Iraqis Practice Gasoline Rationing

They didn't tell us very much, and what they did tell us, we already knew a month ago. If you had gone to sleep for a month and then had awakened in that room, you would have thought you had just taken a 10-minute nap.

Representative Nancy Pelosi

D-California, on the Bush administration's closed-door briefings for Congress

Okay, Okay – You're Not A Wimp. Can We Go Home Now?

Anti-war saying

Bluntly put: war now or war later.

Daniel Pipes

Director of the Foreign Policy Research Institute

I eat my way through a crisis.

First Lady Barbara Bush

<u>**Q:**</u>

Percentage of African-American soldiers in the Persian Gulf War

<u>**A:**</u>

20

<u>**Q:**</u>

Percentage of African-American soldiers in the Vietnam War

<u>**A:**</u>

10

<u>**Q:**</u>

Percentage of African-American soldiers in World War II

<u>**A:**</u>

9

October 29-31

Iraq invaded and we all asked, 'Where is the army?' We realized then that we don't really have one.

Saudi royal adviser

For the moment, there are not many reasons for optimism.

Eduard Shevardnadze

Soviet Foreign Minister

I love freedom. When I get out of this and go home, I'll go to the beaches and have a nice swim.

Clem J. Hall

Educator from Maryland held hostage in Iraq

The American flag is flying over the Kuwaiti Embassy and our people inside are being starved by a brutal dictator ... I have had it with that kind of treatment of Americans.

President Bush

Marines Practice On Oman Beach

81 House Democrats Oppose Offensive Action To Force Iraq Out Of Kuwait

All the Americans at sites have complete freedom. They can watch TV, read books and read newspapers. They also enjoy the friendship of Iraqi forces.

Latif Jassim

Iraq's Minister of Culture and Information

Drift, muddle and confusion are beginning to replace the confident spirit of August.

Senator Malcolm Wallop

R-Wyoming

[*The* United States and Britain] have no respect for human values.

Iraqi Foreign Ministry

Q:

General Schwarzkopf's monthly salary

A:

$8,485.80 plus $942 housing and dependency allowance

Q:

Estimated amount Bantam Books promised General Schwarzkopf for the world rights to his planned book

A:

Over $5,000,000

SPECIAL DOCUMENT:
Mobilization Orders

FROM: Commandant of the Marine Corps
TO: Capt. Stephen Bucy
    0537461393/ IRR Member

SUBJ: Orders to extended active duty

REF: (A) Title 10 (USC)

1. You are ordered to extended active duty under the provisions of the reference which authorizes your recall to active duty in the event of declared national emergency or war. Failure to report will be considered absence without leave and you may be subject to judicial action under the uniform code of military justice.

REPORT TO: Marine Corps Mob Station   (MCC:SFP)

RPT DATE: 91/02/09

Following initial screening at the mobilization station, you will proceed to your station of initial assignment (SIA) and report by 2400 on the date shown below.
SIA: Replacement Battalion West 4 (MCC: 014)
GAINING COMMAND: MWHS 3   (MCC: 143)
SIA ARRIVAL DATE: 91/02/11

2. The following items will be required upon reporting to the mobilization station:
        All military uniforms
        Military ID card
        Copy of marriage certificate
        Copies of divorce decrees for both yourself and wife (if applicable)
        Copies of birth certificates for your dependent children
        Other legal documents which you may feel necessary
                for the purpose of determining dependency

And Their Cancellation

All life insurance policy information (name/address
of the insurance company and policy number).

3. You will receive all pay and allowances that accrue to an active duty Marine of
your grade/years of service. For the duration of Operation Desert Storm, all travel
and duty associated with your activation is considered temporary duty. You will be
eligible for per diem in accordance with current regulations when not in a field duty
status. The following items are required in order to authorize Variable Housing
Allowance (VHA) for your home of record ...

4. If you are physically incapacitated by serious illness or injury and cannot report
you must immediately furnish the OIC of the mobilization station a physician's
statement giving an estimate of the time required to return to limited or full duty. If
you are able to report and found not physically qualified, your orders will be
endorsed and you will be directed to return to your home ...

WESTERN UNION MAILGRAM

FROM: Commandant of the Marine Corps
TO: Stephen Bucy
0537461393/ IRR Member

SUBJ: Orders to extended active duty

REF: (A) Title 10 (USC)

1. Your orders to active duty have been cancelled. This notice supercedes any
previously received Mailgram.

2. Unfortunately you were erroneously sent mobilization orders. We regret any
inconvenience or apprehension this action may have caused you or your family.

November

The mother of all battles is nearer today.

November 1-4

When a democracy marches off to war, it should be able to explain itself in 25 words or less.

Neal B. Freeman

National Review magazine

They have committed outrageous acts of barbarism. Brutality – I don't believe that Adolf Hitler ever participated in anything of that nature.

President Bush

on Iraqi troops

Please do not forget the guest hostages.

U.S. hostage letter smuggled out of Iraq

You have to make it as clinical and efficient as possible.

Senior British defense official

on a possible war with Iraq

I would describe myself as owlish – wise enough to understand that you want to do everything possible to avoid war – that once you're committed to war, then be ferocious enough to do whatever is necessary to get it over as quickly as possible in victory.

General Schwarzkopf

Baker Mideast Tour Lays Foundation For Military Operation

When the great military confrontation takes place, the Gulf region will return a half-century back ... the Americans and other warmongers will be preoccupied with nothing but searching for remnants of their dead bodies.

Iraq's government newspaper Al Jumhuriya

This is an island of a man, who has really both isolated and insulated himself from the entire rest of the world.

General Schwarzkopf

on Saddam Hussein

Kuwait is Arabic for Vietnam

Saying at protest rally

I know what I'm facing when I step in that boxing ring. They don't have any idea what's in store for them.

Boxer Thomas "Hit Man" Hearns

to American soldiers

The battle is not over what happened August 2. The battle is over the Palestinian issue.

Saddam Hussein

Q:

Number of meetings Secretary of State James Baker had with foreign dignitaries between August 2, 1990 and January 15, 1991

A:

200

November 5-8

This is a long, long way from home, but I think that Americans are at home wherever our principles are.

Secretary of State James Baker

The American people will ... ask him why he is sending their sons to be killed in the Arab desert, and he will reap the fruits of his mistake.

Latif Jassim

Iraq's Minister of Culture and Information, referring to President Bush

"When are we going to get to go home?"

"How long have you been here?"

"Too long."

Exchange between enlisted woman and Secretary of State James Baker

Time is running out for Saddam Hussein.

Margaret Thatcher

Prime Minister of Great Britain

We have done everything we can do. The answer from the Iraqi Government has been insults and dirty words against me. Either he doesn't realize the tremendous forces being arrayed against him, or his aides are misleading him or not telling him.

Hosni Mubarak

President of Egypt

230,000 U.S. Troops In Gulf Region

European Community Pledges Unity

U.S.S. Midway Enters Persian Gulf

I want to tell you as a member of the leadership, we will never go out of Kuwait, ever.

Latif Jassim

Iraq's Minister of Culture and Information

Congress has a moral and institutional obligation to rein in the dogs of war at this critical moment.

Representative Ronald Dellums

D-California

Mr. Secretary, as your fellow Texan Lyndon Johnson used to say, 'Never tell a fellow to go to hell unless you mean to send him there.'

Prince Bandar bin Sultan

Saudi ambassador speaking to Secretary of State James Baker

[*Thatcher's*] continued calls for beating the drums of war show beyond a shadow of a doubt that this woman ... has lost her mental balance.

Latif Jassim

Iraq's Minister of Culture and Information

As far as I am concerned, I would like my country to be liberated today and before tomorrow.

Sheik Juber al-Ahmed al-Sabah

Emir of Kuwait

Q:

Percentage of the total oil they each require that France, Italy, and Japan import from the Persian Gulf

A:

35%, 32%, 64%

November 9-12

*O*ur rotation plan has just become a reinforcement plan.

Lieutenant Colonel Fred Peck

Marine Corps spokesman

*W*e're going to give them the most violent three to five minutes they've ever seen.

Marine Major General Royal N. Moore

*I*t's really scary because George Bush has painted himself into a corner with those troop movements and nothing I've seen has indicated that he's man enough to back out.

James Packer

Vietnam veteran and leader of Veterans for Peace

*T*he mother of all battles is nearer today. If the fire of aggression is unleashed against Iraq, flames will cover everything, will be over everything, and will burn everything in every direction.

Iraq's government newspaper Al Jumhuriya

Bush Calls Up 240,000 U.S. Troops

U.S. Abandons Gulf Troop Rotation Plan

Hussein Dismisses Military Chief Of Staff

We know a war is a war. Some of us won't make it back. But we say, 'let's do it so the rest of us can go home.'

Marine Sergeant Frank Huerta

Nobody's coming out.

Senior military official

on the U.S. military's plan to not rotate Gulf troops

War is not discouraged by running away from it any more than criminals are discouraged by the absence of police.

Tom Clancy

Author of "The Hunt for Red October"

Barriers are serious obstacles only to tactical bozos.

Military historian

on Iraq's mines and fortifications

FACT:

Sailors serving with the Royal Navy in the Persian Gulf used money they received for donating blood to telephone home to wives and sweethearts.

Q:

Number of coups d'etat in Iraq between 1920 and 1979, when Saddam Hussein ascended to the presidency

A:

13

November 13-16

If George Bush wants his presidency to die in the Arabian desert, he's going at it very steadily and as if it were a plan.

Senator Daniel Patrick Moynihan

D-New York

We know that Kuwait is going to be ruined, but it's better to have a liberated but destroyed Kuwait than an undestroyed but occupied Kuwait.

Abdallah Bishara

Leader of the Gulf Cooperation Council

I wish I would've told you 'no.'

Wife of National Guard member

who asked her permission before signing up

My parents are threatening to break my foot or my arms so I can't go.

Arthur Watkins

National Guard member

Let the wimps step aside. I'll go in their place.

65-year-old Howard d'Amico

What the lunch-pail guy wants to know is, Can I drive my car and will the [New England] Patriots be on the tube Sunday?

Clyde Mark

Middle East specialist

Senators Ask Bush To Convene Emergency Session Of Congress

Bush Begins Eight-Day Trip To Gulf Region And Europe

You want to be the tough female officer who can handle any mission, and it makes me really proud to see so many women out here showing they are made of the right stuff. But, oh God, I do miss my children, my husband and the sweet rhythms of family life.

*Major
Susan Alderson*

We wouldn't have troops there if the resource was guano.

Ted Van Dyk

*Democratic party
consultant*

We're mercenaries, bought and paid for.

*Sergeant
Gary Farmer*

in Saudi Arabia

I'm in the military. If they say I go, I go. I do not want to debate the President. But it won't hurt anyone's feelings if they cancel this flight.

*Sergeant
Bill Walton*

FACT:

WAR WORDS:

<u>BCDs</u>:

'Birth Control Device' glasses, ugly military issue spectacles

<u>Chocolate Chips</u>: Desert camouflage uniforms

<u>Get your gut right</u>: Eat

<u>Homers</u>: Iraqi commanders; after Bart Simpson's Dad

Q:

Amount paid by the United States to Iraq for oil between 1983 and 1989

A:

$5,500,000,000

November 17-20

It's 1990, we're on the brink of World War III, and Saudi Arabia has just formally banned driving by women. It's crazy. It's sad. It's ridiculous.

Professional woman

in Saudi family

The peace movement took a long time clearing its throat. But now it's finding its voice, and I think it will be heard.

Reverend William Sloane Coffin

President of SANE/Freeze

For Saddam Hussein, this overbuildup is like pushing a rat into a corner. Eventually, like any wild animal, he'll jump, and that's worrisome.

Richard Legal

30-year-old carpenter from Florida

These Colors Don't Run

Saying on T-shirt

depicting the American flag

We're not anti-military; we're just anti-misuse of the military.

Stephen C. Sossaman

Vietnam veteran opposing the Gulf buildup

It would be the first war in history where ground forces supported air forces.

Retired Marine Lieutenant General Bernard E. Trainor

Iraq Vows Christmas Hostage Release
"Imminent Thunder" Landings Continue
Iraq To Commit 250,000 More Troops

It's the ultimate irony: women may lose their lives defending a sexist society.

Lynne Randall

No support at home: that's what a lot of us would find hardest to take.

Lance Corporal Christopher Bost

President Bush just seems so embarrassing. He's goofed up so many other things, I think people are reluctant to follow him into battle.

Joseph Sobran

National Review magazine

They're balking at cold, hard cash because it has all kinds of overtones. It is the mercenary aspect.

Lawrence J. Korb

explaining the reluctance of the Allies to pay for Operation Desert Shield

FACT:

Baghdad Betty, an Iraqi radio personality, has tried to demoralize U.S. troops, sometimes warning them that Kuwaiti sheiks were wooing their wives back home.

Q:

Amount a cousin of Saudi Arabia's King Fahd lost at casinos on the French Riviera in August

A:

$21,640,000

November 21-25

If push comes to shove, we're going to get Roseanne Barr to go to Iraq and sing the national anthem.

President Bush

joking with the troops in Saudi Arabia

I want to go home! This isn't our war! What are we doing here? Why are we over here? We aren't supposed to be here – this isn't our war!

Two American soldiers shouting at reporters

With every passing day Saddam is one step closer to realizing his goal of a nuclear arsenal .... Your mission is marked by a real sense of urgency.

President Bush

speaking to the troops in Saudi Arabia

Anyone who believes this can be solved militarily must think of the end, not the beginning of the enterprise.

Helmut Kohl

German Chancellor

Kuwait is our land. This is something we are taught by our grandfathers.

Jubir Musasaadom

Iraqi English teacher

Bush Shares Thanksgiving Dinner With Troops In Saudi Arabia

Britain To Double Its Gulf Troop Force

He must get out of Kuwait and we're not joking about that. This is not comedy hour in the Security Council.

Yuli P. Vorontsov

Soviet representative to
the United Nations

If you want to sum it up in one word, it's jobs.

Secretary of State
James Baker

stating one possible
explanation for why U.S.
troops were sent to the Gulf

War is a very solemn and sobering and extraordinary act, and the decision to go to war should not be granted to one person.

Representative
Ronald Dellums

D-California

If anybody imagines that he can undermine Iraq and he can attack Iraq, I say, go and drink the center of the sea.

Iraq's official
Thanksgiving
message

FACT:

On November 21,
45 House Democrats
filed a lawsuit to bar
President Bush from
taking offensive
action in the Persian
Gulf without
obtaining a
Congressional
declaration of war.

Q:

Estimated number
of times that a U.S.
President has sent
troops into combat
situations

A:

130

November 26-30

We are lighting our own fuse.

Senator Sam Nunn

D-Georgia, Chairman of the Senate Armed Forces Committee, on the U.S. military buildup

Victory in this war will be ashes in the mouth of the victor.

Yasser Arafat

Chairman of the Palestine Liberation Organization

I'm here because I have a 22-year-old son. As long as there are people that profit from wars then there will be wars. The only thing that happens in wars is that people get used.

Jerry Rau

Vets for Peace member at protest vigil

It's curious that some expect our military to train soldiers to stand up to hostile fire but doubt its ability to train them to occupy ground and wait patiently.

Admiral William J. Crowe

Former Chairman of the Joint Chiefs of Staff

If you put a dozen intelligence experts around a conference table and ask them to tell you when Iraq will have a [nuclear] bomb, you'll get a dozen answers, from six months to ten years.

U.S. government expert

Saddam Hussein represents a new phenomena in Arab societies – a man who is tough, obstinate, and resolute under tremendous pressure.

Abdel Karim al-Iryani

Foreign Minister of Yemen

I remember asking the recruiter if we would ever be shipped out to war, and he said, 'No, you can volunteer if you want.' Stupid me, I believed him.

Colin Bootman

Reservist seeking discharge

He's a very nice man, very sincere. I got all teary during the meeting, and President Hussein had to ask one of his aides to get me some Kleenex.

Mary Trundy

Sister of one of the hostages

I just refuse to believe that a third-world person who rides a camel can be as smart as I am.

Dave Leppelmeier

F-18 pilot, on Iraqi pilots

Q:

Number of gallons of water U.S. soldiers in the Gulf must drink daily to prevent dehydration

A:

6

Inappropriate Songs

This partial list of songs "with lyrics that need thought in scheduling," was sent by the British Broadcasting Corporation to music programmers at the BBC's local radio stations. The stations were advised that broadcasting these songs might be "inappropriate or hurtful" in light of the ongoing Gulf War. The final play/no play decision was left to the local programmers.

ARTIST	SONG
Abba	*Under Attack*
The Alarm	*68 Guns*
The Animals	*We Gotta Get Out of This Place*
Joan Baez	*The Night They Drove Old Dixie Down*
Bangles	*Walk Like an Egyptian*
Pat Benatar	*Love Is a Battlefield*
Big Country	*Fields of Fire*
Blondie	*Atomic*
Kate Bush	*Army Dreamers*
Cher	*Bang Bang (My Baby Shot Me Down)*
Eric Clapton	*I Shot the Sheriff*
Phil Collins	*In the Air Tonight*
Elvis Costello	*Oliver's Army*
Cutting Crew	*I Just Died in Your Arms Tonight*
Desmond Dekker	*Israelites*
Dire Straits	*Brothers in Arms*
Duran Duran	*View to a Kill*

José Feliciano	*Light My Fire*
Fire Choice	*Armed and Extremely Dangerous*
Roberta Flack	*Killing Me Softly*
Elton John	*Saturday Night's Alright For Fighting*
John Lennon	*Give Peace a Chance*
	Imagine
Bob Marley	*Buffalo Soldier*
Billy Ocean	*When the Going Gets Tough*
Donny Osmond	*Soldier of Love*
Paper Lace	*Billy Don't Be a Hero*
Queen	*Killer Queen*
	Flash
Tom Robinson	*War Baby*
The Specials	*Ghost Town*
Bruce Springsteen	*I'm on Fire*
Edwin Starr	*War*
Status Quo	*In the Army Now*
Cat Stevens	*I'm Gonna Get Me a Gun*
Tears for Fears	*Everybody Wants to Rule the World*
10cc	*Rubber Bullets*
Stevie Wonder	*Heaven Help Us All*

Source: *Harper's* magazine, April 1991

December

*I feel extremely
lonely.*

December 1-3

War is mankind in its most ludicrous state.

Lieutenant General Charles Horner

Commander of Desert Shield Air Force operations

I feel extremely lonely. I have not been this worried in decades.

Henry Kissinger

Former U.S. Secretary of State

[President Bush] gave Saddam Hussein what he really wanted – to be accepted by the mighty as an equal.

Tahseen Bahshir

Egyptian commentator

Let us be clear-eyed about our hopes that the sanctions will make war unnecessary: suffering children are part of our objective.

George F. Will

Washington Post newspaper

We will not permit our troops to have their hands tied behind their backs ....
If one American soldier has to go into battle, that soldier will have enough force behind him to win.

President Bush

Bush Invites Aziz To Washington, Offers To Send Baker To Baghdad

Iraq Accepts Offer Of Baker Visit

I am going to use every single thing that is available to me to bring as much destruction to the Iraqi forces as rapidly as we possibly can in the hopes of winning victory as quickly as possible.

General Schwarzkopf

*I*raqi soldiers enter a home, tie up the men, rob the valuables and then rape the women. Most of the women I saw were molested and then sodomized.

Doctor in Kuwait

The President is going an additional mile, but going the true extra mile means giving sanctions time to work.

Senator Edward M. Kennedy

D-Massachusetts

FACT:

Iraq created a new government department to produce a biography immortalizing President Saddam Hussein.

Q:

Annual trade in 1983 and 1989 between the United States and Iraq

A:

$571,000,000 and $3,600,000,000 (a seven-fold increase)

December 4-6

If You Don't Support Our President And Our Country Get Out.

Counter demonstrator saying

by Operation Desert Shield supporter

I have no question about the competence and ability of our United States Air Force to inflict terrible punishment.

General Colin Powell

Chairman of the Joint Chiefs of Staff

Many troops in Saudi Arabia are shoveling sand into envelopes and sending it home as souvenirs — but it often leaks out, grinding up postal machinery.

Peter Grier

Christian Science Monitor newspaper

Being a liar, he claimed that war with Iraq would be quick .... The thing that Bush must understand clearly is that a war with Iraq is not a picnic in the backyard of the United States.

Iraq's government-run newspaper Al-Thawra

Iraq Offers To Free Soviet Hostages

Baker Appears Before Senate Foreign Relations Committee

It would soon be time to fish or cut bait, as you say.

Senior British government official

on the January 15 deadline

It is better for us to deal with him now than it will be for us to deal with him 10 years from now.

Secretary of Defense Richard Cheney

on Saddam Hussein

You can flatten Iraq. But American planes will not be safe in the sky, and you will need five bodyguards for every American in the Mideast.

Mohammed Milhen

Palestine Liberation Organization

The use of force is equivalent and tantamount to war, and war is tantamount to destruction, desolation and death.

Gonzalo Aquirre

Vice President of Uruguay

Q:

Distance a non-nuclear aircraft carrier travels on one gallon of fuel, in feet

A:

17

Q:

Distance that the battleship U.S.S. Missouri can send a shell weighing 1,900 pounds (comparable to a small car), in miles

A:

23

December 7-9

I don't care about face. He doesn't need any face. He needs to get out of Kuwait.

President Bush

We're going to party naked on the roof and pour champagne on our heads.

Terry Louisbury

Canadian hostage, on being told of his release

By releasing the hostages and offering to talk about everything, he is creating irresistible pressure for negotiations. I fear we lack the political gumption to attack him under those circumstances.

U.S. official

on Saddam Hussein

If there is a war, we ought to be able to look at the family member of somebody who gets killed and say it was worth it, and we exhausted all the other options.

Senator Sam Nunn

D-Georgia, Chairman of the Senate Armed Forces Committee

Iraq Agrees To Free All Hostages

U.S. To Vacate Kuwait Embassy

I'm afraid the children are the unsung victims of Operation Desert Shield. There's no question that women can do this. The question is whether we should.

Lori Moore

Former sergeant, after her general discharge for deciding to stay with her children

You see some of them sitting there in the aisles crying their eyes out. The shock of their husbands going to Saudi is hitting some of them very hard.

Army family counselor

in Germany

I do have this great faith that this will all be resolved in a rational manner, but of course, what's rational to you may not be rational to me.

Lieutenant General Charles Horner

Commander of Desert Shield Air Force Operations

FACT:

Saddam Hussein's favorite movie is "The Godfather"

Q:

Number of square feet in Aspen, Colorado home owned by Saudi Ambassador to the United States Prince Bandar bin Sultan

A:

55,000

Q:

Number of bedrooms in the home

A:

28

December 10-16

It's like M*A*S*H except we can't change the channel.

Staff Sergeant Mike Quick

*H*eaven help the small countries who are fighting for freedom and democracy and have no oil!

Alfred Sumanas

Lithuanian-American Club of Central Florida

Some of the people guarding us were frightened to death. They had been told that their throats would be slit if any of us escaped, and it was probably true.

Stuart Williams

Banker from New York and hostage

The sentiment of business leaders is that the United States shouldn't be holding a gun to the head of Saddam Hussein. There are a lot of other ways to influence his behavior.

Kazuo Nukuzawa

Managing director of Keidanren, a Japanese trade association

The looming war ... is, according to ... the President's men, a sequel to World War II, a full-employment program, a recession buster, a unilateral disarmament campaign and a way to force democracy and women's liberation on Arabia Deserts.

Daniel Singer

The Nation magazine

American Hostages In Baghdad Evacuated
Iraq Says It Wants 'Deep Dialogue' With The U.S.
U.S. And Iraq Cannot Agree On Date For Talks

Saddam Hussein is not too busy to see … Kurt Waldheim, Willy Brandt, Muhammad Ali, Ted Heath, John Connally, Ramsey Clark and many, many others on very short notice. And it simply is not credible that he cannot, over a two-week period,

(continued)

make a couple of hours available for the Secretary of State.

President Bush

Freedom is not free. You have to pay for it sometimes …

Sergeant First Class Lemorris Grover

Army recruiter

Bush will face a divided public if in fact we go to war. There is by no means a consensus. It depends on the circumstances and to some degree on the spin put on the situation.

Frank Newport

Gallup Poll

Washington is acting like a man who works feverishly to fix the sink while the rest of the house is burning out of control.

Rami G. Khouri

Host of a current affairs show on Jordanian television

Q:

World rank of the Soviet Union, the United States and Saudi Arabia in production of oil

A:

1, 2, 3

December 17-24

Iraq does not bend before the storm.

Saddam Hussein

*I'*m not in a negotiating mood.

President Bush

*It'*s a kind of fatalism. People already are dying emotionally and psychologically – so it is not such a threat for them to die physically.

Iraqi reservist

*There'*s a doctor that many in this community need and depend on, and they're sending him to Germany to handle the runny noses of servicemen's kids.

Charles Dahlin

Utah resident

'Negotiations' is not a bad word. Either you negotiate a diplomatic settlement or you have a war.

Senator Paul Simon

D-Illinois

Short of bullets flying, mail is the most important thing going on here.

Larry Bullock

U.S. military postmaster

A partial withdrawal would reward aggression.

Secretary of State James Baker

God is on our side. That is why we will beat the aggressor.

Saddam Hussein

I can't pretend it's Christmas out in the desert. I just can't pretend that well.

Private Deborah Sharpley

FACT:

Eight American soldiers were poisoned by home-brewed alcohol and hospitalized ... one in very serious condition.

Associated Press

I felt ashamed of my government because they never expressed a clear opinion or stated their principles.

Kumiyasi Nakagami

Japanese hostage

If we get into an armed situation, he's going to get his ass kicked.

President Bush

Q:

Percentage of U.S. Gulf Crisis television coverage between August 8, 1990 and January 3, 1991 that dealt with popular opposition to the United States buildup

A:

1%

December 25-31

*M*ay leaders be convinced that war is an adventure with no return.

Pope John Paul II

in his Christmas message "To the City and the World"

*T*here's real sandlot ball over there.

Major Bill Lurenta

*B*y January 15, we'll be 150 percent ready and raring to go. We'll be sending Saddam a couple of Christmas gifts if he doesn't get his act together.

Technical Sergeant Ricardo Febles

Weapons specialist

*T*he Bush Administration ought to have more faith in its diplomatic skills. Saddam's pledge to release hostages is pretty good evidence that you don't have to pull the trigger to get his attention.

Senator Christopher Dodd

D-Connecticut

*I*raq is ready for serious and constructive dialogue based on mutual respect, but rejects the trend of arrogance, vanity and the imposition of will which the American government tries to use.

Saddam Hussein

Hussein Threatens Attack On Tel Aviv

U.S. Soldiers Inoculated Against Biological Weapons

We believe that the initiation of offensive military action by the United States unwisely risks massive loss of life.

Representative George Miller

D-California, with 109 House members in a letter to President Bush

Kuwaitus Interruptus – Pull Out Now!

Anti-war saying

I don't want to see another Vietnam in the Persian Gulf. We don't want our men and women to die in a senseless war. This is not about naked aggression; it's about oil.

Ron Kovic

Antiwar activist and author of "Born on the Fourth of July"

He must have been drunk, and drunk people usually lose their senses.

Latif Jassim

Iraq's Minister of Culture and Information on Bush's suggestion that Iraq withdraw from Kuwait

FACT:

The Salvation Army sent two mobile canteens to the Gulf to supply British forces with tea and snacks.

Q:

Amount of liquid nerve gas required to kill a person

A:

1 pinhead-sized drop

President Bush's Letter

Mr. President:

We stand today at the brink of war between Iraq and the world. This is a war that began with your invasion of Kuwait; this is a war that can be ended only by Iraq's full and unconditional compliance with U.N. Security Council Resolution 678.

I am writing you now, directly, because what is at stake demands that no opportunity be lost to avoid what would be a certain calamity for the people of Iraq. I am writing, as well, because it is said by some that you do not understand just how isolated Iraq is and what Iraq faces as a result.

I am not in a position to judge whether this impression is correct; what I can do, though, is try in this letter to reinforce what Secretary of State Baker told your Foreign Minister and eliminate any uncertainty or ambiguity that might exist in your mind about where we stand and what we are prepared to do.

The international community is united in its call for Iraq to leave all of Kuwait without condition and without further delay. This is not simply the policy of the United States; it is the position of the world community as expressed in no less than 12 Security Council resolutions.

We prefer a peaceful outcome. However, anything less than full compliance with U.N. Security Council Resolution 678 and its predecessors is unacceptable.

There can be no reward for aggression. Nor will there be any negotiation. Principle cannot be compromised. However, by its full compliance, Iraq will gain the opportunity to rejoin the international community.

More immediately, the Iraqi military establishment will escape destruction. But unless you withdraw from Kuwait completely and without condition, you will lose more than Kuwait.

What is at issue here is not the future of Kuwait – it will be free, its government will be restored – but rather the future of Iraq. This choice is yours to make.

The United States will not be separated from its coalition partners. Twelve Security Council resolutions, 28 countries providing military units to enforce them, more

To Saddam Hussein

than 100 governments complying with sanctions – all highlight the fact that it is not Iraq against the United States, but Iraq against the world.

That most Arab and Muslim countries are arrayed against you as well should reinforce what I am saying; Iraq cannot and will not be able to hold on to Kuwait or exact a price for leaving.

You may be tempted to find solace in the diversity of opinion that is American democracy. You should resist any such temptation. Diversity ought not to be confused with division. Nor should you underestimate, as others have before you, America's will.

Iraq is already feeling the effects of the sanctions mandated by the United Nations. Should war come, it will be a far greater tragedy for you and your country.

Let me state, too, that the United States will not tolerate the use of chemical or biological weapons or the destruction of Kuwait's oil fields and installations. Further, you will be held directly responsible for terrorist actions against any member of the coalition.

The American people would demand the strongest possible response. You and your country will pay a terrible price if you order unconscionable acts of this sort.

I write this letter not to threaten, but to inform. I do so with no sense of satisfaction, for the people of the United States have no quarrel with the people of Iraq.

Mr. President, U.N. Security Council Resolution 678 establishes the period before January 15 of this year as a "pause of good will" so that this crisis may end without further violence.

Whether this pause is used as intended, or merely becomes a prelude to further violence, is in your hands, and yours alone. I hope you weigh your choice carefully and choose wisely, for much will depend on it.

George Bush

Source: *Minneapolis Star Tribune* newspaper, January 13, 1991

BRITISH FLIGHT LIEUT. JOHN PETERS

LIEUT. COLONEL CLIFFORD ACREE

ITALIAN CAPTAIN MAURIZIO COCCIOLONE

KUWAITI PILOT MOHAMMED MUBARAK

IRAQI TV

IR 01.5

4
3
2
1

January

*It looks like
the Fourth
of July.*

January 1-6

Everybody ready?

Vice President of the United States, Dan Quayle

visiting troops in Saudi Arabia

Everything has already been settled. Iraq took over a country, and we're going to take it back.

Specialist Jeff Roberts

The crocodile tears shed by Hosni for those of us who fall as martyrs are to no avail, since martyrdom is the highest rung that can be reached by an Iraqi or Arab person.

The official Iraqi News Agency

on Egyptian president Hosni Mubarak

Stop Bush from destroying Iraq in order to award Kuwait to the sultans of Saudi Arabia and Texas.

Melvin Salo

St. Louis Park, Minnesota

The United States is becoming the weapon of choice.

James Webb

Former U.S. Secretary of the Navy

Heads will turn white, cities will collapse and the mutilated bodies of victims will be scattered in seas of blood.

Hosni Mubarak

President of Egypt

If Saddam does his calculations, he will see he has no chance.

Jacques Poos

Foreign Minister of Luxembourg

Dan Quayle Visits Middle East Troops

Bush Proposes Gulf Talks In Switzerland; Iraq Agrees To Talks

Of course there are problems. They totally freaked out the first time they saw a woman driving a forklift.

Army Lieutenant David Colson

on Saudi soldiers

They have my phone number.

Joseph Wilson

U.S. Charges d'Affairs in Baghdad on the Bush administration's interest in a dialogue with Iraqis

Saddam Hussein doesn't think we have the stomach for conflict, and to listen to American officials say this almost every day feeds his appetite.

Senator Richard Lugar

R-Indiana

I have respect for Mr. Bush, but I do not feel I am in the position of a second-class soldier who must obey his commanding general.

Francois Mitterand

President of France, on French peace initiatives

They're 3-to-1 against immediate military action. In other words, no war now.

Senator George Mitchell

D-Maine, on the opinion of his constituency

Q:

Number of American women stationed in the Gulf as of January 1, 1991

A:

25,000

January 7-10

What bothers me is that they don't want any entertainment – and they still invited me.

Bob Hope

on the Saudi government

We used to fight for what we needed, then we fought for what we wanted, now we fight for what we waste.

Ralph Nader

Consumer advocate

When a head of state writes to another head of state a letter and he really intends to make peace, he should use polite language.

Tariq Aziz

Foreign Minister of Iraq,
after rejecting Bush's
letter to Hussein

Mr. Minister, I want to ask you one more time, are you sure that you do not want to receive this letter?

*Secretary of State
James Baker*

to Tariq Aziz, Foreign
Minister of Iraq

A peace is better to win than a war.

*Richard J.
Cattani*

Editor,
Christian Science Monitor
newspaper

Bush Seeks War Resolution From Congress

U.S.-Iraq Talks In Switzerland Fail

Mr. Bush, we are the children of Iraq! We are the soldiers of President Saddam Hussein! Listen, Mr. Bush, you are stealing our milk and food! But we are strong, and we will fight you!

Samir Mowfaq

10-year-old

Your alliance will crumble and you will be left lost in the desert. You don't know the desert because you have never ridden on a horse or a camel.

Tariq Aziz

Foreign Minister of Iraq to Secretary of State James Baker

If the Americans only give them one alternative – surrender or fight – then I believe they will enter the war.

Senior Soviet envoy

on the Iraqi options

Who am I to tell kings what to do? They're busy people. It's a wonderful gesture he's coming out here now.

General Schwarzkopf

on King Fahd's finally coming to visit U.S. troops

Q:

Chances that an Iraqi male between the ages of 15 and 39 was a soldier in the Gulf War

A:

1 in 3

January 11-13

... let us come together after the vote with the notion that we are Americans here, not Democrats and not Republicans ... without anything but the solemn cry that on this great decision day we voted as our conscience and judgment told us we should.

Representative Thomas Foley

D-Washington

I have yet to meet a mother or a father who would send their son and daughter into battle for a twenty-cent differential in the price of regular unleaded.

Representative Mike Synar

D-Oklahoma

It is awesome. You hit that button, and death is on the way.

Colonel Jerry "Gunner" Laws

If the Americans attack it will be the most suicidal thing.

Izzat Ibrahim

Vice-Chairman, Iraq's Revolutionary Command Council

Just so there is no misunderstanding, let me be absolutely clear: We pass the brink at midnight, January 15.

Secretary of State James Baker

I can't wait. It may be the day you can legally kill somebody.

Private First Class Jerry Smith

Congress Debates War Resolutions

Congress Authorizes Use Of Force To Remove Iraq From Kuwait

In case of war be sure that our very first target will be Israel.

Tariq Aziz
Foreign Minister of Iraq

Sir, you understand, all the stuff we told you about liking it here, we only said that because our commanders told us we had to.

Soldier's private comment to reporter

I do not believe the administration has made this case to go to war. And if I apply this standard to my children, then I have to apply this standard to everyone's children.

Senator Paul Wellstone

D-Minnesota

When we should have been debating, we were on vacation. Now that we should be quiet, we want to vote.

Senator Robert Dole

R-Kansas, dismissing a call by Democrats for a full debate on the Gulf crisis

FACT:

Less than a week before war broke out, Mr. Hussein ordered the traditional Muslim warrior's cry "Allah Akhbar" or "God is greater" emblazoned on the Iraqi flag.

Q:

Number of members of Congress whose son or daughter served in the Persian Gulf

A:

7

January 14

The War Is Only A Symptom!

Anti-war saying

Iraq is a good car with a bad driver. Maybe now we change driver.

Baghdad resident

This SCUD's for you.

Twist on Budweiser slogan

Ever since I was a kid, I've wanted to fly choppers. I could have been a jet pilot, but there's nothing like being close to the troops in my own bird.

Major David Johnson

463rd Helicopter Squadron

We SHELL not EXXONerate Saddam Hussein for his actions. We will MOBILize to meet this threat to vital interests in the Persian GULF until an AMOCOble solution is reached. Our best strategy is to BPrepared. FINAlly, we ARCOming to kick your ass.

Statement

circulating at oil companies

Israel Promises Retaliation In Case Of An Iraqi Attack

U.N. Leader Meets With Hussein And Aziz

I'd Fly 10,000 Miles To Smoke A Camel

Saying on T-shirt

I think we are talking about a war of weeks as opposed to months.

Representative Les Aspin

D-Wisconsin, Chairman of the House Armed Services Committee

The worst-case scenario in their eyes is that he says 'yes' and withdraws.

Edward Luttwak

Military strategist, on U.S. fears of a partial Iraqi withdrawal

This is the best chance for peace.

Senator Robert Dole

R-Kansas, on empowering the President to go to war

WILL WAR IMPACT SNOW-BOARDING?

Headline

Snowboard Industry News magazine

FACT:

Workers who make bedsheets for babies also made 16,099 body bags for possible deaths in Operation Desert Shield.

Q:

Amount enlisted American military personnel with less than two years of experience can expect to earn for one year's enlistment

A:

Between $13,656 and $21,800 including base pay and a typical food allotment and housing allowance

January 15

The shortest route home is through Baghdad.

Air Force colonel

Why do we allow a handful of men to decide the fate of thousands?

Jane Wingate

Minneapolis Star Tribune newspaper

I do want to stay, and I think it's safe as long as I don't go to McDonalds with 20 other Americans and sing Yankee Doodle Dandy.

Katie Spring

Wellesley College exchange student in Madrid, Spain

Our troops are there to stay forever. Kuwait is the 19th province of Iraq and there is no way that this will change. The issue of Kuwait is finished.

Latif Jassim

Iraq's Minister of Culture and Information

At least four weddings are taking place in Jeddah after the ticking of mid-night hour of January 15, which signals that whatever is looming, optimism is booming.

Mohammed Alis al-Jifri

Saudi Gazette newspaper

The U.N.-Endorsed Deadline For Iraqi Withdrawal From Kuwait Passes

You have an expression in English – 'You need two to tango' – and I wanted very much to dance, but I didn't find a nice lady to dance with.

Javier Perez de Cuellar

Secretary General of the United Nations, on the failure of negotiations in Baghdad

At midnight today, the world will cross the bridge, with Saddam not yet showing any willingness not to get drowned in the river of blood beneath.

Saudi Gazette newspaper

It is appalling that Martin Luther King's birthday should be used as the date when George Bush says this country is going to war.

Barry Romo

Vietnam Veterans Against the War

FACT:

U.S. forces in the Gulf hold no religious services. Instead, they have 'P-morale meetings,' 'C-morale meetings' and 'J-morale meetings.'

Q:

Number of times that the U.S. Congress has declared war

A:

5

January 16

The liberation of Kuwait has begun.

Marlin Fitzwater

White House Press Secretary

Tonight the battle has been joined.

President Bush

There is a fatal moment where one must act. This moment, alas, has arrived.

Michel Rocard

Prime Minister of France

I think it is time for me to express deep sorrow.

Javier Perez de Cuellar

Secretary General of the United Nations

I had a brother who was a medic in Vietnam and when he came home all he wanted to do was sit in the dark, drink beer and listen to sad music ... Two years later, he committed suicide. I don't want that to happen to other young men.

June Hanson

Minneapolis, Minnesota artist

My confidence in you is total. Our cause is just! Now you must be the thunder and lightning of Desert Storm.

General Schwarzkopf

speaking to American troops

This guy is the closest thing to Hitler since Hitler himself.

Army Sergeant Myron Block

War Begins

I appreciate your support for impeachment of the President because of Operation Desert Shield ... I introduced a Resolution of Impeachment of the President on January 16th.

Representative Henry Gonzalez

D-Texas, in reply to a supporter

It's a volunteer military, it's their choice to be in, and now it's time to pay up. But that doesn't make it any easier.

Air Force Lieutenant Colonel Doug Cole

It is about power and commitment. On both sides, the greatest fear is being seen to be a wimp.

Fouad Ajami

Director of Middle East Studies at Johns Hopkins University

✝

There come times when we must fight for peace. I pray we will be on God's side.

Reverend Billy Graham

Q:

Amount that Iraq, Great Britain and France spent for arms procurement between 1980 and 1990

A:

$105,000,000,000
$69,500,000,000
$68,600,000,000

January 16

Bull's Eye.

Headline

The Argus
newspaper

I felt like I
was on the
50-yard line
of a football
game, yelling
'Go! Go!
Go!'

*Major
Robert Leonik*

Apache Pave Low
helicopter pilot watching
the entire Allied Air Force
stream through a corridor
he helped create through
Iraqi air defenses

We dropped
the bombs
and ran like
hell. It was
absolutely
terrifying.
There is no
other word
for it.
We were
frightened
of failure,
frightened
of dying.

*Lieutenant Ian
Long*

British flyer, Royal Air
Force, 31st Tornado
Squadron

It was lit up
like a huge
Christmas
tree.

Air Force pilot

upon returning from the
first mission over Baghdad

You pick
precisely
which target
you want ...
the men's
room or the
ladies' room.

*Colonel
Alton Whitley*

Commander of a wing of
F-117A stealth fighters

We stay
ready and
we stay
together.
So when we
come at you,
we'll come as
one, all mean
and nasty.
That's why
we call
ourselves the
Nasty Boys.

Ricky Cantrell

Commander, 2nd Marine
Division, 8th Tank
Battalion

The great
battle has
begun.

Iraqi State Radio

War Begins

The glorious sons of our nation are in a battle of justice against vice, of the believers against the infidels.

Saddam Hussein

Clearly I've never been there, but it feels like we are in the center of hell.

Bernard Shaw

CNN anchorman on the bombing of Baghdad

We're going to go deep [behind Iraqi lines] using aerial assets and challenge them in ways seen and unseen [Hussein] never dreamed of.

General Colin Powell

Chairman of the Joint Chiefs of Staff

Hell no, we won't go. We won't kill for Texaco.

Anti-war saying

The sky is lighting up to the south with anti-aircraft fire and red and flashes of yellow light … there's another attack coming in … It looks like the Fourth of July.

Peter Arnett

CNN correspondent in Baghdad

Some people ask, 'why act now?' The answer is clear. The world could wait no longer.

President Bush

Q:

Percentage of Americans with TVs who watched President Bush declare war

A:

79% (second all-time to the 81% who watched President Kennedy's funeral)

January 17

We're into euphoria control around here.

U.S. presidential adviser

The guy's doing a rope-a-dope on us.

U.S. strategist

on Saddam Hussein

My calls were 20 to 1 in favor of the war. It was amazing. Leading up to the war, they were running 3 to 1 against. I've never seen a turnaround so fast.

Gil Gross

Radio talk show host

What they expect Israel to do is a retaliation, kind of an eye-for-an-eye, tooth-for-a-tooth retaliation ... or maybe two eyes for an eye, the way Israel does it.

Representative Les Aspin

D-Wisconsin, Chairman of the House Armed Services Committee, on Iraqi expectations

The only thing I'm afraid of is chemical warfare. Other than that, I'm not scared at all .... we're really not worried about him.

John Wohlford

Father of Tyrone Wohlford, tank mechanic

Speak for yourself.

Dory Wohlford

Mother of Tyrone Wohlford, tank mechanic

Iraqi SCUDs Launched Into Israel And Saudi Arabia

Crude Oil Prices Take Biggest One-Day Fall In History

I locked him in, confirmed that he was hostile, and fired a missile ... It was a huge fireball. I feel good. I never experienced this before.

Captain Steve Tate

F-15 fighter pilot

I joined the military to help me, not to kill me.

Masked AWOL soldier

in Minneapolis, Minnesota

It spent 14 hours in my underpants, so it's a little bit sweaty.

Sebastian Rich

British cameraman on smuggling out the first video of the bombing of Baghdad

It's like a Redskins game when it starts out really well and you're scared they'll blow it.

Sheerah Roache

Washington, D.C., referring to the Washington Redskins professional football team

*O*peration Desert Storm may be a success for advanced military technology, but the resort to war reflects a failure for the human spirit.

The National Council of Churches

*T*he time is nigh ... to get rid of ... the Satan in the White House, the whole nest in the White House, and the poisonous whole nest in Tel Aviv.

Saddam Hussein

Q:

Number of seconds in which a SCUD missile can fly one mile

A:

Under 1

January 18-19

When there is an alarm we spend our time in the sealed room drawing helicopters, bombs and Saddam Hussein.

Hamutal Niv

Israeli 5-year-old

It will be continuous; it will be all-out; it will be awesome.

Senator Alan Simpson

R-Wyoming, on the Allied bombing

When Bernard Shaw went off the air for CNN, the whole room exploded in cheers.

Lieutenant General Charles Horner

Commander of Desert Storm Air Force Operations, on monitoring the progress of first wave bombing of Baghdad's TV station and seeing that Iraq's communications network had been hit

Before we pull their teeth we're going to have to pluck out their eyes and plug their ears.

U.S. military official

The Americans will come here to perform acrobatics like Rambo movies.

Saddam Hussein

There don't seem to be any civilian casualties .... Buildings are being taken out in populated areas without damaging adjoining structures.

Peter Arnett

CNN correspondent in Baghdad

If it flies, it dies.

Patriot missile crew saying

More Iraqi SCUDs Hit Israel

Patriot Antimissile Missiles Shipped To Israel

When the air-raid sirens go off, everybody starts looking at the sky instead of the road. Saddam Hussein's most fearsome weapon of the war's first week was the unguided Chevrolet Caprice Classic sedan.

P.J. O'Rourke

Rolling Stone magazine

Americans are dying and Iraqis are dying, and what are we doing talking about our periods and going shopping? But when you get up there, you saw how much people had to laugh.

Nicole Niemi

Comedian

He said the time for debate is over. I told him that the thing that distinguishes us from Nazi Germany and Iraq is that we allow the debate to continue.

Jennifer Leazer

University of Minnesota student on her confrontation with a man tearing down war protest signs

George Bush has drawn his rifle. He cannot back down.

Fouad Ajami

Director of Middle East Studies at Johns Hopkins University

Q:

Total number of Iraqi SCUD ballistic missile attacks on Israel and Saudi Arabia

A:

81

January 20-21

I think our leaders and our people have wrongly attacked the peaceful people of Iraq.

Lieutenant Jeffrey Zaun

Captured Navy aviator, speaking in a monotone

He's alive, he's alive! He's a tough son of a bitch. He's a survivor .... [The Iraqis] are putting words into his mouth.

Calvin Zaun

Lieutenant Zaun's father

America is angry about this. If [Hussein] thought this brutal treatment of pilots is the way to muster world support, he is dead wrong.

President Bush

The human garbage of the American peace movement will have found a way to blame their country for the hostilities .... The world will never be the nuclear-free petting farm the peace movement likes to portray.

Robert K. Brown

Editor/Publisher, Soldier of Fortune magazine

Allied POWs Displayed On Iraqi Television

I am just 21 years old and I have spent almost my whole life with wars. I've seen children die in front of my eyes. And now I am supposed to lose my whole family in war? Don't American people understand that we are human too?

Zainab Rasheed
of Baghdad

*W*ithout alcohol and other diversions, these troops just may be the toughest ever. Saddam might just regret having given us time to get ready.

Sergeant
First Class
Donna Munyon

*T*wo things people should not watch are the making of sausage and the making of war.

Air Force doctor
William Burner

FACT:

A man in Bangladesh hacked his son to death because the young man believed Iraqi President Saddam Hussein could not win the war against allied forces.

Q:

Distance an M-1 tank travels on one gallon of fuel, in miles

A:

.56

January 22-24

*O*ur strategy for dealing with this army is very simple: First we're going to cut it off, then we're going to kill it.

General Colin Powell

Chairman of the
Joint Chiefs of Staff

*I*t was my day.

Captain Ayedh al-Shamrani

Saudi pilot who shot down
two Iraqi fighter planes
in one day

They say that you could fire one of these Tomahawk Cruise missiles off in Boston Harbor and send it through the goalposts in RFK Stadium in Washington, D.C., and have a better field goal percentage than Chip Lohmiller.

Bob Zelnick

ABC-TV correspondent
comparing the accuracy of
the Cruise missile and the
Washington Redskins'
placekicker

No one should weep for this tyrant when he is brought to justice – no one, anywhere in the world.

President Bush

Kuwaitis were the most corrupt people on earth. They used to make weddings for their cats.

Sheik Tamimi

of the Jordanian extremist
group Islamic Holy War

Nobody can be John Wayne. They can always find a torture so grave you'll confess to something.

Dr. Robert Rabe

on POWs

The obvious question to many is why, instead of going to discos, don't they enlist?

Ahmed al-Nafisi

Former member of Kuwaiti
Parliament, in Cairo, on
young Kuwaiti men

When we start having ground losses and Americans start seeing the Emir of Kuwait and his 80 wives on television and we see the Kuwaiti and Saudi students driving fancy cars at our local community colleges, a lot of people are going *(continued)*

to be very unhappy.

*Representative
Patricia
Schroeder*

D-Colorado

If you think spilling oil is a disaster, wait until we start spilling blood.

*Greenpeace
Action
advertisement*

I have no doubt about God now. I am closer to Him and my inner self. You think about how you will be remembered if you bite the big one.

*Lance Corporal
Henderson J.
Nugent*

What do the Iraqis have in common with Lisa Olson? They've both seen Patriot missiles up close.

Victor Kiam

*Owner of the New England
Patriots professional
football team, on the female
reporter before whom
several Patriot players
allegedly exposed themselves*

Q:

*Distance under
Baghdad Saddam
Hussein reportedly
has a German-built,
nuclear-proof luxury
bunker, in feet*

A:

80

January 25-27

I for one will not weep for him.

John Major

Prime Minister of
Great Britain referring
to the possibility of
Saddam Hussein's death

You can't say 'King Fahd's a donkey and we want to eat the Americans,' and then turn around and ask for aid.

Lawyer

in Amman, Jordan

American soldiers have an absolutely intuitive, Donkey Kong-based, gut level understanding of the technology being used to fight this war. Thank God they grew up in video arcades. That's why we're winning.

P.J. O'Rourke

Rolling Stone magazine

We could make it so the Iraqis are using gas lamps for the next 100 years.

Israeli military official

Europe is an economic giant, a political dwarf and a military worm.

Mark Eyskens

Foreign Minister of Belgium

We cannot deal with it. If winds and tides are unkind, Bahrain may be swamped by an ocean of oil.

Jawad al-Arrayed

Health Minister of Bahrain

They will be submerged parking lots.

John W. Tunnell, Jr.

Professor, Corpus Christi
State, predicting shore
conditions from Saudi
Arabia to Bahrain as
a result of oil spill
accumulations

*B*aghdad will be bright and sunny, with lows in the mid-40s and highs in the upper 10,000s. Winds will be from the south, southeast and southwest at 1,500 to 1,800 knots. Sunscreen 300 is recommended. Chances of precipitation of molten objects are 90 to 99%.

Messages from the computer underground in Saudi Arabia

I would have killed him if I could, with no more remorse than killing a cockroach.

Bob Simon

captured CBS correspondent on one of his Iraqi guards

✡

*W*e have said from the start that if attacked, we will respond.

Benjamin Netanyahu

Depuly Foreign Minister of Israel

It's hard to kill someone, but if he becomes an enemy, he deserves it.

Captain Ayedh al-Shamrani

Saudi pilot

I just wish Hussein was the champion of the world and I was the challenger— it'd be about a 15-second round.

Frank Sinatra

Singer

*T*hey're the war channel. It's war, more war, all war.

Howard Stringer

President of the CBS Broadcast Group, on CNN's coverage

Q:

Estimated size of the Gulf oil spills, in barrels

A:

1,500,000

Q:

Estimated size of the Exxon Valdez oil spill off the Alaskan coast, in barrels

A:

260,000

January 28-31

I don't want to die for my country. I'd rather that some Iraqi die for his country.

Jeff Shapiro

Navy enlistee

About as significant as a mosquito on an elephant.

General Schwarzkopf

on the Iraqi capture of Khafji

*P*eople have to understand that they can't believe a word that a man says in captivity .... There's not a person in the world who can hold out against pain indefinitely.

Lloyd Bucher

Former POW

We know they're there – they probably know we're here .... If you want to stay alive, don't advertise.

First Sergeant Jim Southerly

American scout

We will prevail.

President Bush

The Iraqi army in Kuwait is crumbling like a doughnut that's been soaked in too much coffee.

David Harkworth

Retired paratrooper and author of "About Face"

I was very thirsty. I drank it. To save your life, you risk your life.

Jemis Mut

Baghdad resident, on drinking polluted water

First U.S. Female Soldier MIA

First Large Ground Battle In Khafji

Seven Marines Killed By 'Friendly Fire'

He has plenty hidden away. The Western press lies about his losses. Eventually, Iraq will win. It's sure.

Mazen Barghouti

Jordanian shopkeeper on Saddam Hussein

If he has them, he could use them, but if he uses them, he is risking himself and his country to a very, very grave extent.

Yitzhak Shamir

Prime Minister of Israel, on Saddam Hussein and Iraq's chemical weapons

---

This is going to be the defining moment for America's role in the world for a decade or more to come.

Representative Les Aspin

D-Wisconsin, Chairman of the House Armed Services Committee

I've used 'rested and resolute.' 'Calm and resigned.' 'Determined and vigilant.' 'Steady and strong.'

Marlin Fitzwater

White House Press Secretary, on his 'mood words' for President Bush

---

Hard Luck Cafe: Baghdad – Outdoor Seating Available

T-shirt saying

Waikiki Beach, Hawaii

Q:

Number of allied planes shot down in air-to-air combat during the Gulf War

A:

0

SPECIAL DOCUMENT:
The House Vote

Here is the 250 to 183 roll call by which the House gave President Bush the authority to wage war in the Persian Gulf.

ALABAMA Democrats: Bevill, yes; Browder, yes; Cramer, yes; Erdreich, yes; Harris, yes. Republicans: Callahan, yes; Dickinson, yes.

ALASKA Republican: Young, yes.

ARIZONA Democrat: Udall, not voting. Republicans: Kolbe, yes; Kyl, yes; Rhodes, yes; Stump, yes.

ARKANSAS Democrats: Alexander, no; Anthony, no; Thornton, yes. Republican: Hammerschmidt, yes.

CALIFORNIA Democrats: Anderson, yes; Beilenson, no; Berman, yes; Boxer, no; Brown, no; Condit, yes; Dellums, no; Dixon, no; Dooley, no; Dymally, not voting; Edwards, no; Fazio, no; Lantos, yes; Lehman, yes; Levine, yes; Martinez, no; Matsui, no; Miller, no; Mineta, no; Panetta, no; Pelosi, no; Roybal, no; Stark, no; Torres, no; Waters, no; Waxman, no. Republicans: Campbell, yes; Cox, yes; Cunningham, yes; Dannemeyer, yes; Doolittle, yes; Dornan, yes; Dreier, yes; Gallegly, yes; Herger, yes; Hunter, yes; Lagomarsino, yes; Lewis, yes; Lowery, yes; McCandless, yes; Moorhead, yes; Packard, yes; Riggs, no; Rohrabacher, yes; Thomas, yes.

COLORADO Democrats: Campbell, yes; Schroeder, no; Skaggs, no. Republicans: Allard, yes; Hefley, yes; Schaefer, yes.

CONNECTICUT Democrats: DeLauro, no; Gejdenson, no; Kennelly, no. Republicans: Franks, yes; Johnson, yes; Shays, yes.

DELAWARE Democrat: Carper, yes.

FLORIDA Democrats: Bacchus, yes; Bennett, no; Fascell, yes; Gibbons, no; Hutto, yes; Johnston, no; Lehman, no; Peterson, no; Smith, no. Republicans: Bilirakis, yes; Goss, yes; Ireland, yes; James, yes; Lewis, yes; McCollum, yes; Ros-Lehtinen, yes; Shaw, yes; Stearns, yes; Young, yes.

GEORGIA Democrats: Barnard, yes; Darden, yes; Hatcher, yes; Jenkins, no; Jones, yes; Lewis, no; Ray, yes; Rowland, yes; Thomas, yes; Republican: Gingrich, yes.

HAWAII Democrats: Abercrombie, no; Mink, no.

IDAHO Democrats: LaRocco, no; Stallings, no.

ILLINOIS Democrats: Annunzio, no; Bruce, no; Collins, no; Costello, no; Cox, no; Durbin, no; Evans, no; Hayes, no; Lipinski, no; Poshard, no; Rostenkowski, yes; Russo, no; Sangmeister, no; Savage, no; Yates, no. Republicans: Crane, yes; Fawell, yes; Hastert, yes; Hyde, yes; Madigan, yes; Michel, yes; Porter, yes.

INDIANA Democrats: Hamilton, no; Jacobs, no; Jontz, no; Long, no; McCloskey, no; Roemer, no; Sharp, no; Visclosky, no. Republicans: Burton, yes; Myers, yes.

IOWA Democrats: Nagle, no; Smith, no. Republicans: Grandy, yes; Leach, yes; Lightfoot, yes; Nussle, yes.

KANSAS Democrats: Glickman, yes; Slattery, yes. Republicans: Meyers, yes; Nichols, yes; Roberts, yes.

KENTUCKY Democrats: Hubbard, yes; Mazzoli, no; Natcher, no; Perkins, no. Republicans: Bunning, yes; Hopkins, yes; Rogers, yes.

LOUISIANA Democrats: Hayes, yes; Huckaby, yes; Jefferson, no; Tauzin, yes. Republicans: Baker, yes; Holloway, yes; Livingston, yes; McCrery, yes.

MAINE Democrat: Andrews, no. Republican: Snowe, yes.

MARYLAND Democrats: Byron, yes; Cardin, no; Hoyer, no; McMillen, yes; Mfume, no. Republicans: Bentley, yes; Gilchrest, yes; Morella, no.

MASSACHUSETTS Democrats: Atkins, no; Donnelly, no; Early, no; Frank, no; Kennedy, no; Markey, no; Mavroules, no; Moakley, no; Neal, no; Studds, no. Republican: Conte, no.

MICHIGAN Democrats: Bonior, no; Carr, no; Collins, no; Conyers, no; Dingell, yes; Ford, no; Hertel, no; Kildee, no; Levin, no; Traxler, no; Wolpe, no. Republicans: Broomfield, yes; Camp, yes; Davis, yes; Henry, yes; Pursell, yes; Upton, yes; Vander Jagt, yes.

MINNESOTA Democrats: Oberstar, no; Penny, no; Peterson, no; Sabo, no; Sikorski, no; Vento, no. Republicans: Ramstad, yes; Weber, yes.

MISSISSIPPI Democrats: Espy, no; Montgomery, yes; Parker, yes; Taylor, no; Whitten, yes.

MISSOURI Democrats: Clay, no; Gephardt, no; Horn, no; Skelton, yes; Volkmer, yes; Wheat, no. Republicans: Coleman, yes; Emerson, yes; Hancock, yes.

MONTANA Democrat: Williams, no. Republican: Marlenee, yes.

NEBRASKA Democrat: Hoagland, yes. Republicans: Barrett, yes; Bereuter, yes.

NEVADA Democrat: Bilbray, yes. Republican: Vucanovich, yes.

NEW HAMPSHIRE Democrat: Swett, yes. Republican: Zeliff, yes.

NEW JERSEY Democrats: Andrews, no; Dwyer, no; Guarini, no; Hughes, yes; Pallone, yes; Payne, no; Roe, no; Torricelli, yes. Republicans: Gallo, yes; Rinaldo, yes; Roukema, yes; Saxton, yes; Smith, yes; Zimmer, yes.

NEW MEXICO Democrat: Richardson, no. Republicans: Schiff, yes; Skeen, yes.

NEW YORK Democrats: Ackerman, yes; Downey, no; Engel, yes; Flake, no; Hochbrueckner, no; LaFalce, no; Lowey, no; Manton, no; McHugh, no; McNulty, yes; Mrazek, no; Nowak, no; Owens, no; Rangel, no; Scheuer, no; Schumer, no; Serrano, no. Slaughter, no; Solarz, yes; Towns, no; Weiss, no. Republicans: Boehlert, yes; Fish, yes; Gilman, yes; Green, yes; Horton, yes; Houghton, yes; Lent, yes; Martin, yes; McGrath, yes; Molinari, yes; Paxon, yes; Solomon, yes; Walsh, yes.

NORTH CAROLINA Democrats: Hefner, no; Johnes, yes; Lancaster, yes; Neal, no; Price, no; Rose, no; Valentine, yes. Republicans: Ballenger, yes; Coble, yes; McMillan, yes; Taylor, yes.

NORTH DAKOTA Democrat: Dorgan, no.

OHIO Democrats: Applegate, no; Eckart, no; Freighan, no; Hall, no; Kaptur, no; Luken, yes; Oskar, no; Pease, no; Sawyer, no; Stokes, no; Traficant, no. Republicans: Boehner, yes; Gillmor, yes; Gradison, yes; Hobson, yes; Kasich, yes; McEwen, yes; Miller, yes; Oxley, yes; Regula, yes; Wylie, yes.

OKLAHOMA Democrats: Brewster, yes; English, no; McCurdy, yes; Synar, no. Republicans: Edwards, yes; Inhofe, yes.

OREGON Democrats: AuCoin, no; DeFazio, no; Kopetski, no; Wyden, no. Republican: Smith, yes.

PENNSYLVANIA Democrats: Borski, yes; Coyne, no; Foglietta, no; Gaydos, no; Gray, no; Kanjorski, no; Kolter, no; Kostmayer, no; Murphy, no; Murtha, yes; Yatron, no. Republicans: Clinger, yes; Coughlin, yes; Gekas, yes; Goodling, yes; McDade, yes; Ridge, yes; Ritter, yes; Santorum, yes; Schulze, yes; Shuster, yes; Walker, yes; Weldon, yes.

RHODE ISLAND Democrat: Reed, no. Republican: Machtley, yes.

SOUTH CAROLINA Democrats: Derrick, yes; Patterson, yes; Spratt, yes; Tallon, yes. Republicans: Ravenel, yes; Spence, yes.

SOUTH DAKOTA Democrat: Johnson, no.

TENNESSEE Democrats: Clement, yes; Cooper, yes; Ford, no; Gordon, yes; Lloyd, yes; Tanner, yes. Republicans: Duncan, yes; Quillen, yes; Sundquist, yes.

TEXAS Democrats: Andrews, yes; Brooks, yes; Bryant, no; Bustamante, no; Chapman, yes; Coleman, no; de la Garza, yes; Edwards, yes; Frost, yes; Geren, yes; Gonzalez, no; Hall, yes; Laughlin, yes; Ortiz, yes; Pickle, no; Sarpalius, yes; Stenholm, yes; Washington, no; Wilson, yes. Republicans: Archer, yes; Armey, yes; Bartlett, yes; Barton, yes; Combest, yes; DeLay, yes; Fields, yes; Smith, yes.

UTAH Democrats: Orton, yes; Owens, no. Republican: Hansen, yes.

VERMONT Independent: Sanders, no.

VIRGINIA Democrats: Boucher, no; Moran, no; Olin, no; Payne, yes; Pickett, yes; Sisisky, yes. Republicans: Bateman, yes; Bliley, yes; Slaughter, yes; Wolf, yes.

WASHINGTON Democrats: Dicks, no; Foley, no; McDermott, no; Swift, no; Unsoeld, no. Republicans: Chandler, yes; Miller, yes; Morrison, yes.

WEST VIRGINIA Democrats: Mollohan, yes; Rahall, yes; Staggers, no; Wise, no.

WISCONSIN Democrats: Aspin, yes; Kleczka, no; Moody, no. Obey, no. Republicans: Gunderson, yes; Klug, yes; Petri, yes; Roth, yes; Sensenbrenner, yes.

WYOMING Republican: Thomas, yes.

Associated Press   Source: *Washington Post* newspaper, January 13, 1991

The Senate Vote

Following is the 52 to 47 vote by which the Senate empowered President Bush to use U.S. armed forces to expel Iraq from Kuwait:

DEMOCRATS FOR

Breaux (La.), Bryan (Nev.), Gore (Tenn.), Graham (Fla.), Heflin (Ala.), Johnston (La.), Lieberman (Conn.), Reid (Nev.), Robb (Va.), Shelby (Ala.).

REPUBLICANS FOR

Bond (Mo.), Brown (Colo.), Burns (Mont.), Chafee (R.I.), Coats (Ind.), Cochran (Miss.), Cohen (Maine), Craig (Idaho), D'Amato (N.Y.), Danforth (Mo.), Dole (Kan.), Domenici (N.M.), Durenberger (Minn.), Garn (Utah), Gorton (Wash.), Gramm (Tex.), Hatch (Utah), Heinz (Pa.), Helms (N.C.), Jeffords (Vt.), Kassebaum (Kan.), Kasten (Wis.), Lott (Miss.) Lugar (Ind.), Mack (Fla.), McCain (Ariz.), McConnell (Ky.), Murkowski (Alaska), Nickles (Okla.), Packwood (Ore.), Pressler (S.D.), Roth (Del.), Rudman (N.H.), Seymour (Calif.), Simpson (Wyo.), Smith (N.H.), Specter (Pa.), Stevens (Alaska), Symms (Idaho), Thurmond (S.C.), Wallop (Wyo.), Warner (Va.).

DEMOCRATS AGAINST

Adams (Wash.), Akaka (Hawaii), Baucus (Mont.), Bentsen (Tex.), Biden (Del.), Bingaman (N.M.), Boren (Okla.), Bradley (N.J.) Bumpers (Ark.), Burdick (N.D.), Byrd (W. Va.), Conrad (N.D.), Daschle (S.D.), DeConcini (Ariz.), Dixon (Ill.), Dodd (Conn.), Exon (Neb.), Ford (Ky.), Fowler (Ga.), Glenn (Ohio), Harkin (Iowa), Hollings (S.C.), Inouye (Hawaii), Kennedy (Mass.), Kerrey (Neb.), Kerry (Mass.), Kohl (Wis.), Lautenberg (N.J.), Leahy (Vt.), Levin (Mich.), Metzenbaum (Ohio), Mikulski (Md.), Mitchell (Maine), Moynihan (N.Y.), Nunn (Ga.), Pell (R.I.), Pryor (Ark.), Riegle (Mich.), Rockefeller (W.Va.), Sanford (N.C.), Sarbanes (Md.), Sasser (Tenn.), Simon (Ill.), Wellstone (Minn.), Wirth (Colo.).

REPUBLICANS AGAINST

Grassley (Iowa), Hatfield (Ore.).

NOT VOTING

Cranston (D-Calif.).

Associated Press *Washington Post* newspaper, January 13, 1991

Early War Timetable

Here is an hour-by-hour account of events as war began today in the Persian Gulf. All times are local time in the gulf.

12:50 a.m.
First F-15E fighter-bombers take off in pairs from the largest U.S. air base in central Saudi Arabia.

2:40 a.m.
ABC and CNN television news report "flashes in the sky" over Baghdad and say tracer fire appears to be coming from the ground.

2:56 a.m.
The U.S. military announces that war with Iraq began as a squadron of U.S. fighter-bombers took off from the U.S. air base in Saudi Arabia.

3:06 a.m.
White House issues statement by President Bush confirming that "forces were engaging targets in Iraq and Kuwait."

5:00 a.m.
President Bush addresses the nation announcing the decision to attack Iraq and Kuwait and says, "We will not fail."

5:30 a.m.
Defense Secretary Richard Cheney and General Colin Powell, Chairman of the Joint Chiefs of Staff, tell Pentagon reporters that hundreds of U.S. and Allied warplanes launched predawn strikes in Iraq and Kuwait and met "no air resistance" from Iraq.

Associated Press   Source: *Minneapolis Star Tribune* newspaper, January 17, 1991

WESLEY—

February

*You didn't
move it and
now you'll
lose it.*

February 1-2

We as Americans no longer tend to glorify war. We lost a lot of that in Vietnam.

John Shulimson

Marine Corps historian

We have discovered that it is possible to be against war – to think that it is not going to solve anything – and at the same time to want to smash Saddam ...

Michael Lerner

Editor of Tikkun, a liberal Jewish journal

We were here for Thanksgiving, Christmas, New Year's. Now we're here for the Super Bowl.

Major Jim Miller

of Anaheim, California

I feel like a parent who has done everything to prepare kids for challenges, but you can't stay with them to help them cope.

Army Captain Keith George

3rd Armored Division

*I*raq won the toss and elected to receive.

Roadsign

in Cincinnati, Ohio on Super Bowl Sunday

The American computer can never defeat the virtuous spirit of Iraq.

Saddam Hussein

Like a 'special operations theme park.'

U.S. official

on activities of U.S. Special Forces troops

The big difference between this anti-war movement and the Vietnam one is the presence of a big, strong negative symbol in Saddam Hussein. It was possible to portray Ho Chi Minh as a native revolutionary working for independence.

(continued)

Saddam Hussein is armed with biological and chemical weapons, and is very effectively presenting himself as a very bad guy.

Robert Loevy

Political scientist, Colorado College

I think what he wants is to inflict casualties, be chased out of Kuwait, then declare victory.

Steven Spiegel

Christian Science Monitor newspaper

I'm not going to fight his war. He's going to fight our war.

General Schwarzkopf

Saddam Hussein doesn't make it easy to be against the war.

Senator Paul Wellstone

D-Minnesota

Q:

Number of Americans killed in Vietnam

A:

58,173

February 3-5

Remember, that guy on the other side has some problems. The poor devil has been living in a hole under constant bombing.

Army Captain Keith George

3rd Armored Division

Before I left, my father wasn't ready to talk much about his experiences. Now, I kind of have my own little Vietnam here. When I go home, maybe we can start talking.

Specialist Joe Vasquez

of Canby, California

America will be defeated. Like us, the Iraqis are fighting on their own territory, which gives them a high fighting spirit. Secondly, they were well prepared for the war and they can learn from Vietnam's experiences.

Tring Hoang

61-year-old Hanoi, Vietnam resident

EFFORT TO NAME SON SCUD IS TORPEDOED

Headline

Minneapolis Star Tribune newspaper

My nightmare is anything that would cause mass casualties among my troops. I don't want my troops to die. I don't want my troops to be maimed.

General Schwarzkopf

One B-52 Crashes In The Indian Ocean

Iranian President Rafsanjani Offers To Hold Direct U.S.-Iraq Talks

I just think this is too much to ask of one mother. Five sons are too many for one mother to give.

Minnie Pearl Jornett

of Memphis, Tennessee, mother of five soldiers

He initiated the war, and now he wants us to pray for peace.

Rick Mingory

on President Bush's call for a day of prayer

I've known a lot of generals who were war lovers. They scare the living hell out of me, and they're also not very good generals, not by my measure. Custer loved war, and look what he accomplished.

General Schwarzkopf

Nobody who is going to go face to face with the Iraqis – cold steel to cold steel – believes it will be a cakewalk. Nobody here is saying that we'll be home by Easter.

Michael Steele

Marine helicopter pilot

Q:

Number of stars on the uniforms of Generals Powell and Schwarzkopf

A:

4

Q:

Number of stars on the uniforms of Generals George Marshall, Douglas MacArthur, Dwight Eisenhower, Henry Arnold and Omar Bradley

A:

5

February 6-10

Tomorrow if you don't surrender we're going to drop on you the largest conventional weapon in the world.

Leaflet warning Iraqi soldiers of an upcoming attack

Sir, the blokes have just nuked Kuwait!

British SAS commando team

response to the delivery of the above-mentioned bomb

This Saddam Hussein's insane. That's what we call the guy around here: Saddam Insane.

Sergeant Steve Tafoya

Fire rains down upon Iraq ... destroying mosques, churches, schools, museums, hospitals, powdered-milk factories, Bedouin tents, electric-generating stations and water networks.

Saddam Hussein

The Iraqi Armed Forces [will] cover the battlefield with fires that Bush and his allies cannot extinguish.

Iraqi Defense Ministry's daily newspaper Al-Qadissiya

You don't have to bomb cities.

Ramsey Clark

Former U.S. Attorney General

If the enemy sees you before you see him, he's gonna blow your ass off and all the technology in the world is not gonna save you.

First Sergeant John Wright

'*A* sympathizer'

Senator Alan Simpson

R-Wyoming, on CNN correspondent Peter Arnett

We're going up against a lot of our own systems. Today's friend could be tomorrow's enemy. Countries of the world need to be a little more discreet about who they sell weapons to, and that includes us.

Marine Colonel W.L. McMullen

Leader of the "Death Angels" Squadron

I wouldn't mind crawling across the border and doing open heart surgery on Saddam Hussein without anesthetic.

Lieutenant Commander Mike Mozzetti

Physician

FACT:

Algerian youths changed the traditional Arabic greeting – salaam aleikum, peace be with you – to Saddam aleikum – Saddam be with you.

Q:

Number of wars Peter Arnett has witnessed

A:

16

February 11-13

I was sleeping and suddenly I felt heat and the blanket was burning. I turned to try to touch my mother, who was next to me, but grabbed nothing but a piece of flesh.

Omar Adnan

17 years old, after Allied bombing in which hundreds of Iraqi civilians were killed

We don't know why civilians were at this location, but we do know that Saddam Hussein does not share our value in the sanctity of life.

Marlin Fitzwater

White House Press Secretary

'To Saddam: You didn't move it and now you'll lose it. Colin Powell.' 'To Saddam, with affection. Dick Cheney. Def. Sec.'

Notes inscribed on a bomb by General Colin Powell and Secretary of Defense Richard Cheney

We had a list. We crossed off number one, number two, number three, number four. We're hitting everywhere.

Air Force Colonel John McBroom

on Allied bombing targets

There's still a target-rich environment down there.

Lieutenant General Charles Horner

Commander of Desert Storm Air Force Operations

Hussein Offers To Discuss Peace With The Soviet Union

Bombing Raid Kills Hundreds Of Iraqi Civilians

Pray God that this war will end. This war is not good for anybody.

Sae Hussein

Bahraini taxi driver

If we use tactical nuclear weapons, I think it can be effective in getting this war over in a hurry.

Representative Dan Burton

R-Indiana

I have this image of Saddam Hussein and George Bush sending off their children to kill each other, which is what we're doing. It's so sickening.

Muriel Sibley

Peace activist from Victoria, British Columbia, Canada

I smiled inside. When your heart has gone so hard against someone, you are happy to see him hurt, even if it is your enemy doing it.

Talal Nugali

Saudi aircraft engineer on SCUD missiles hitting Tel Aviv

It is a strange new feeling for me. I guess you don't really value your country until you've fought to defend it.

Faisal al-Rasheed

Saudi engineer

Q:

The projected year in which Islam will be the second largest faith in the United States, passing Judaism

A:

2000

February 14-15

I am glad to see the word 'withdrawal' has entered into Kuwait's vocabulary. Perhaps if we wait a bit longer, the word 'Kuwait' will enter into Iraq's vocabulary.

David Hannay

British ambassador to the United Nations

I sew a flag on my uniform. They burn the flag. And then they try to tell me they support me!

U.S. soldier

on anti-war protesters supporting the troops but denouncing the war

Spend more than an hour at the Joint Information Bureau and you begin calling the staircase 'a foot-impelled bidirectional vertical transport asset.'

P.J. O'Rourke

Rolling Stone magazine

They can't get through ... You're guaranteeing me that, right?

General Schwarzkopf to Lieutenant General Charles Horner

on a possible Iraqi fighter plane assault into Saudi Arabia

Regrettably, the Iraq statement now appears to be a cruel hoax.

President Bush

on Iraqi proposal to withdraw

Iraq Offers Conditional Withdrawal

U.N. Security Council Debates War In First Closed Door Session In 15 Years

It was about as heavy as you can get and still be conventional.

U.S. Army Special Forces officer

on the most recent bombing

It kind of looks like Safeway on payday – they're just lining up. We own the skies.

Colonel Gary Voellger

on American planes in Operation Desert Storm

He needs the media not just to polish the good side of the coin, but to hide the ugly face of a killer .... I remember him saying, 'Compared to tanks, journalists are cheap – and you get more for your money.'

Egyptian editor

on Saddam Hussein awarding the "Saddam" prize for journalistic excellence

I don't care if the Palestinians end up in Israel, or in the seas or in hell .... Saddam sent a SCUD on my children and Arafat applauded.

Saudi newspaper editor

FACT:

Combat unit and equipment nicknames include
"Camel Killers,"
"Angel of Death,"
"Atomic Punk,"
"Deliverance,"
"Studs From Hell,"
"Cotton Balers,"
"Hounds of Hell,"
"Bad Attitude,"
"Born to be Wild,"
and
"Brain Damage."

Q:

Total number of U.S. armed forces personnel in the Persian Gulf during the Gulf War

A:

540,000

February 16-17

We hated to come back, but we ran out of bombs.

Air Force Captain Dewey Gay

after a bombing mission

Impeach Bush! Impale Quayle! Draft Neil Bush When He Gets Out of Jail!

Anti-war saying

It'll be everything you ever wanted in a war and never got.

Senior Army officer

on the impending ground war with Iraq

In the beginning I was worried ... but after meeting Saddam I became fully confident of the sound position of Iraq.

Yasser Arafat

Chairman of the Palestine Liberation Organization

Initial Success or Total Failure

Motto of an American bomb-disarming squad

We are obediently absorbing Iraqi missiles night after night. You are withholding from us the right to protect ourselves so that Arab dictators whom you are saving will not, God forbid, be offended. We are a victim of a war that is not ours.

Yoel Marcos

Jewish journalist, in open letter to U.S. Secretary of State James Baker

Kremlin Rejects Iraqi Pullout Proposal

I don't think we should be crucified on this because we have money. The Iraqis are as rich as we are. The only difference is that we dedicated our time and lives to make Kuwait a better place to live and prosper. We didn't invest in military equipment.

Angie Saad

Spokeswoman for Citizens for a Free Kuwait

---

*T*he toilet chain has already been pulled, and Saddam Hussein is about to be flushed away.

Marine Colonel Carl Fulford

*W*e can kill 24 hours a day.

Lieutenant Colonel Tom Stewert

1st Attack Helicopter Battalion, 24th Aviation Brigade

---

*T*o a lot of people, it looks like a war to make the world safe for lounge lizards.

Michael Mandelbaum

Middle East expert at Johns Hopkins University, on affluent and idle Kuwaitis

---

FACT:

The U.S. military dropped more bombs on Iraq in 1 1/2 months than they dropped in 5 years during World War II.

Q:

Number of hours between the Pentagon ordering the manufacture of a "customized bomb" in the United States and that same bomb landing on its target in the Gulf War

A:

36

February 18-20

I've reconciled all the moral issues. It's black versus white, good versus evil.

President Bush

As Napoleon said, you can do anything with bayonets except sit on them.

Robert Stone

Village Voice newspaper

My guys will see their buddy dead alongside the road. They'll stop, they'll cry, they'll puke, and there I'll be behind them, kicking their ass, saying, "Come on, men, we've got a job to do."

Lieutenant Colonel Ron Stewart

The Air Force has been using a kind of scalpel on the Iraqis – cutting here, cutting there, hoping they'll bleed to death. What you see are 10-pound sledges. We'll beat their brains in.

Lieutenant Colonel Dan Merritt

Army tank battalion leader

Medals are often won by people who screw things up at first and then fight like hell to get out of it.

Lieutenant Colonel Dan Merritt

Army tank battalion leader

If you'd kill Saddam, then all this would stop.

Iraqi defector

Soviets Present Peace Plan To Iraq

Mines Damage Two U.S. Ships Off Kuwait

Bush Dismisses Soviet Peace Plan

Those people who say "Let sanctions work" – how can they expect us to live out in the desert like this for one or two years? I'd like to see them live with me here for one month.

Specialist Alan Okke

If he lives, he wins. He will portray his defeat in the Arab world as going 15 rounds with the champion and losing only on points.

Top Israeli official

on Saddam Hussein

Think

THINK BUSH

THINK BUSH THINK

THINK

PEACE

Noel Regalado

Age 10, South Bronx, New York

The true aim behind this devastating war .... is to return Iraq to primitive life. This is a war on all Arabs and Muslims.

King Hussein

of Jordan

Q:

Percentage of residents in Kuwait allowed to vote prior to Iraq's invasion

A:

6%

(adult males able to trace their ancestry to 1920)

February 21-22

✝

If you move forward now you're poking a stick in Gorbachev's eye. The Soviet offer met our basic requirements.

Robert Hunter

Vice president, Center for Strategic and International Affairs

There is an increasing judgement in the churches that the technical sophistication and destruction capacity of modern weapons makes the idea of 'just war' not only obsolete but immoral.

World Council of Churches

We had to learn to rely on ourselves.

Abdullah al-Qabandi

24-year-old Kuwaiti, on taking out the garbage for the first time in his life

I told Jeff Zaun, "You were on the cover of Newsweek ... I expected you to be bigger."

POW First Lieutenant Robert Sweet

of the Air Force 353rd Tactical Fighter Squadron to his fellow captive

We found one guy with dress shoes on – they must've taken him right off the dance floor.

U.S. Army officer

describing the condition of surrendering Iraqis

You could fall asleep and drive for miles, 'cause there's nothing out there.

Specialist Carey Sutterfield

Tank driver, 24th Infantry Division, of Woodward, Oklahoma

Soviet Peace Plan Proposed; Iraq Accepts

U.S. Rejects Soviet Peace Plan

Bush Issues Withdrawal Ultimatum To Iraq

I, therefore, propose a nationwide campaign to get a House resolution passed to have the oil companies in the Gulf area as well as the big defense contractors profiting from the war give a stock bonus to all veterans of the Persian Gulf War.

(continued)

Maybe an extra certificate for knocking out a machine gun or shooting an enemy plane.

Wells Bain

The People magazine

One of our objectives is to humiliate him.

State Department official

on Saddam Hussein

If President Bush does not accept the cease-fire, it will show that his true goal is to destroy Iraq, not liberate Kuwait.

Alana Ramadan

Minneapolis, Minnesota anti-war demonstrator

We live by this teaching: If a man and woman are alone together, the third person present is Satan.

Saudi businessman

Q:

Number of wars in modern history in which Arabs have not been defeated within six days

A:

1

(1991 Gulf War)

February 23-24

Not Wanted Alive

Headline

The European newspaper on Saddam Hussein

Yeah, he might be there. He probably sleeps in the same room with Peter Arnett.

American military officer

on whether Saddam Hussein is using the Al-Rashid Hotel in Baghdad as a base for military operations

My grandfather said that Iraqis will sit at your table and eat your food and smile with you. Then, in the morning, they will steal your sheep while you sleep.

Shad Motari

Kuwaiti electrician

To the final American captive released from Iraq: Turn out the light, bring home the flag. And bring us back the last remaining hostage, the Peace Dividend.

Andrew Kay Lieberman

Los Angeles, California

God bless George Bush! God bless James Baker! God bless Dick Cheney! God bless Margaret Tutwiler!

A liberated Kuwaiti

A madman who suffers from megalomania and the insanity of war.

Baghdad Radio

on President Bush

Allies Launch Ground War Inside Kuwait And Iraq

This is the boringest war I've ever seen ... They just keep dropping their gear and raising their hands.

Sergeant Addison Wembley

on Iraqi troops

It's Vietnam revisited, Vietnam the movie, Part II, and this time it comes out right.

David Tarr

Professor, University of Wisconsin

It brings us back 400 or 500 years. Back to when tribes pillaged each other because one had more than the other.

Suleiman al-Shaheen

Kuwaiti foreign affairs official on Iraq's invasion of Kuwait

VCR's may be made in Japan and Mercedes have their origin, but what's going on in the Middle East is undeniably made in the U.S.A.

Harry Kane

Editor of Operation Desert Shield magazine

If you don't get your legs or your genitals blown off, battle can be very interesting and exciting.

Daniel Ellsberg

Anti-war activist and Vietnam veteran

Q:

Number of times anti-war demonstrator Daniel Ellsberg has been arrested

A:

54

February 25-26

We're going to go around, over, through, on top, underneath and any other way it takes.

General Schwarzkopf

If you can still spit, you're not too nervous to fight.

Warrant Officer Richard Adderton

Orders have been issued to our armed forces to withdraw in an organized manner to the positions they held prior to August 1, 1990.

Baghdad Radio

The war goes on.

Marlin Fitzwater

White House Press Secretary

He asked me at one point, "Am I gonna make it out? Tell me the truth." I said, "No, you're not going to make it outta here." He says, "Don't let me die here." I said, "I'll do my best."

Conversation between Private Frank Bradish of Pocatello, Idaho and a fellow crewman

after their M3A1 cavalry fighting vehicle was hit by enemy fire

If we don't get in soon, this battlefield is going to be one giant ashtray.

Private First Class Chris McCormack

Patchogue, New York

This is the job I came to do. I just hope I don't die of fright before I get there.

Private First Class Jeff McAndrew

Nassau, New Hampshire

Hussein Orders Iraqi Forces Out Of Kuwait
Pentagon Sees War Ending In Days
30,000+ Iraqi Troops Surrender

I don't know. [Burned] women and children all look much the same, don't they?

Pentagon source

on the identity of Iraqi civilians killed inside an air-raid bunker

Our answer has to be, you don't get any reward, except survival.

Senior U.S. official

on Saddam Hussein's proposed diplomatic resolutions

A bogus, puffed-up frog of a man ...

Douglas Hurd

British Foreign Secretary, on Saddam Hussein

I think frankly Saddam is finished. These guys simply don't retire to condos over the Euphrates.

Christine Helms

Middle East scholar

There is space in air-raid bunkers for just one percent of the population of Baghdad ... Now, which one percent do you think is allowed in those bunkers?

Allied government source

FACT:

On the last day of the war, America's elite counterterrorist unit, the Delta Force, helped destroy 26 Iraqi SCUDs that were aimed at Israel.

Q:

Rank "Wind Beneath My Wings" by Bette Midler, "Take This Job and Shove It" by Johnny Paycheck and "God Bless the U.S.A." by Lee Greenwood in number of requests by U.S. soldiers received at Desert Network Radio

A:

1, 2, 3

February 27

Kuwait is liberated. Iraq's army is defeated.

President Bush

Where have you been? We've been waiting for you guys for two weeks!

Iraqi POW officer to his captor

Once we had taken out his eyes we did what could best be described as the 'Hail Mary' play in football.

General Schwarzkopf

No one can find anyone to fight with.

Army Major Bill Powers

on the second day of the ground war

It looks like what's happened is that the mother of all battles has turned into the mother of all retreats.

Secretary of Defense Richard Cheney

Our joy is overflowing, thanks be to God. The enemy is turning tail.

Kuwaiti radio

As far as Saddam Hussein being a great military strategist, he is neither a strategist, nor is he schooled in the operational arts, nor is he a tactician, nor is he a general, nor is he a soldier. Other than that, he's a great military man.

General Schwarzkopf

Resistance Leaders Retake Kuwait City

Bush Halts War

We were 150 miles from Baghdad and there was nobody between us and Baghdad. If it had been our intention to take Iraq ... we could have done it unopposed.

General Schwarzkopf

The Iraqi army is in full retreat.

General Thomas Kelly

I've been kissed by more Kuwaiti men tonight than I can count.

Robert McKeown

CBS correspondent after arriving in Kuwait City

They have been engaged in an epic, valiant battle that will be recorded by history in letters of light.

Saddam Hussein

Soon we will open wide our arms to welcome back home to America our magnificent fighting forces.

President Bush

The jihad has ended ...

Baghdad Radio

on the end of the 'holy war'

The visible smoke plume from Kuwait would cover most of the coastal United States from New York to Florida.

Tom Wicker

New York Times newspaper (July,1991)

Q:

Total number of Kuwaiti oil wells set afire by retreating Iraqi forces

A:

732

February 28

When I left, Kuwait was something like paradise. Now it is something like hell.

Lieutenant Abdulla Mutiri

Kuwait Army Martyr's Brigade

For the first time, there were as many American flags as Confederate at the Daytona 500.

Alan Malamud

Los Angeles Times newspaper

I've never seen anything like this, except in science fiction movies.

Private First Class Orlando Hollins

We're the 911 of the world.

Karen Hall

Mother of Marine Lance Corporal Henry Kolk

It's the climax of George Bush's presidency. It's the climax of his whole life.

Mike McCurry

Democratic strategist

[Morale was] under zero. Bombs 24 hours a day. I cannot take this.

Iraqi Lieutenant Ra'ed Salman

Iraq Promises To Honor All 12 U.N. Security Council Resolutions

I think if we had just fired our guns in the air, the Iraqis would have surrendered.

Kuwaiti Captain Marzook al-Khalifa

I reached back and pieces of my leg were missing.

Private First Class Anthony Drees

recalling SCUD attack on barracks in Dhahran

SADDAM HUSSEIN Imprinted Golf Balls $24.95/dozen

Enjoy Driving That Face 300 Yards

Excellent Gift

Take Out Your Frustration

Product ad

in New York Times newspaper

What I don't plan on doing is ever going to the beach again. I never, never want to see sand again in my life.

Marine Private First Class Tony Morales

FACT:

In July 1991 Arnold Schwarzenegger was the first U.S. civilian to purchase a Humvee all-terrain vehicle. He paid $45,000 and had it customized with a cellular telephone, black leather seats imported from Austria, and an elaborate stereo system. He also had "terminator" painted on both sides.

Q:

U.S. troops killed in the Persian Gulf War

A:

378

SPECIAL DOCUMENT:
Surrender Pamphlet

This pamphlet was air-dropped to Iraqi troops and instructs them on proper surrender techniques.

اوقف القتال الان، حافظ على حياتك

من الملجأ، يجب على حامله التقيد بالخطوات التالية:
للبحث بالسلام
١. اسحب مخزن الذخيرة من سلاحك.
سلاحك على كتفك الايسر مع توجيه الماسورة الى الاسفل.
٢. احمل
٣. ارفع يديك فوق رأسك.
من مواقع القوات المتعددة الجنسيات ببطء وي فرد في
٤. القرب
المقدمة يرفع هذه الوثيقة فوق رأسه.
٥. اذا عملت هذا تنجو من الموت.

CEASE RESISTANCE - BE SAFE

To seek refuge safely, the bearer must strictly adhere to the following procedures:

1. Remove the magazine from your weapon.

2. Sling your weapon over your left shoulder, muzzle down.

3. Have both arms raised above your head.

4. Approach the Multi - National Forces' positions slowly, with the lead soldier holding this document above his head.

5. If you do this, you will not die.

March

By God, we've kicked the Vietnam syndrome

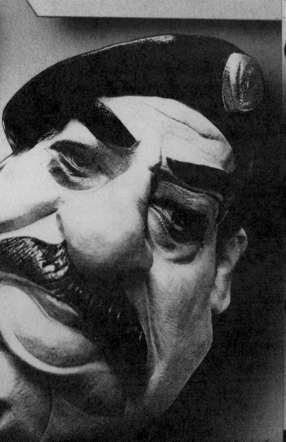

March

Why are we making Saddam Hussein out to be the devil? America and England, we are the devils.

Sinead O'Connor

Singer

Iraq committed grave political errors, which gave the excuse to the imperialist enemy to carry out the first major action as if he were the owner of the world.

Fidel Castro

Perhaps the worst thing that Saddam Hussein has done is allow many Americans to think that nothing has changed.

William Greider

Rolling Stone magazine

Bush sees this New World Order with him on top.

David Blalock

Stop-the-War Brigade, Worms, Germany

Iraq went from the fourth largest army in the world to the second largest army in Iraq in 100 hours.

General Thomas Kelly

We're going to celebrate Thanksgiving, Christmas, Easter and his birthday all in one.

Sidney Welch

on welcoming his son, Airman Apprentice John Stogdale, home to Norfolk, Virginia

Iraq Accepts U.S. Cease-Fire Talk Terms
100,000 Iraqi Casualties Estimated

This is a recent cadaver. You can see his torture. His skull has been smashed, his brains are out, his eyes are gouged out, he has been shot from close range. But he is lucky.... Others you can barely recognize as human.

Dr. Abdul Behbehani

Kuwait City's Mubarak Hospital, on victims of Iraqi torture

You could see them in columns. They looked like little ants in a row coming from a peanut butter and jelly sandwich somebody left on the ground.

Captain John "Smiley" Sizemore

U.S. Air Force pilot, on surrendering Iraqi soldiers

TRADE? Would like to swap pieces of Berlin Wall for pieces of a Patriot. Contact: Jay ARD German TV, ext. 443

Notice posted on bulletin board

Joint Saudi/U.S. Information Bureau, Dhahran

By God, we've kicked the Vietnam syndrome once and for all!

President Bush

Q:

Number of courses on the Vietnam War required for graduation from West Point

A:

0

U.N. Resolutions

Here are the 12 resolutions adopted by the U.N. Security Council between Iraq's invasion of Kuwait on August 2, 1990 and the Gulf War's end on February 27, 1991.

660
Condemns invasion and demands immediate and unconditional withdrawal of Iraqi troops. Passed August 3 (14-0), with Yemen abstaining.

661
Orders trade and financial embargo of Iraq and occupied Kuwait. Passed August 6 (13-0), with Cuba and Yemen abstaining.

662
Declares annexation of Kuwait null and void under international law. Passed August 9 (15-0).

664
Demands that Iraq free all detained foreigners. Passed August 18 (15-0).

665
Allows United States, other naval powers the right to halt shipping to Iraq and Kuwait. Passed August 25 (13-0), with Cuba and Yemen abstaining.

666
Allows humanitarian food aid into Iraq or Kuwait only "to relieve human suffering," as decided by the Security Council. Passed September 13 (13-2), with Cuba and Yemen opposing.

667
Condemns Iraq's aggressive acts against diplomatic missions in Kuwait, including abduction of foreigners. Passed September 16 (15-0).

669

Stresses that only U.N. Sanctions Committee can permit food, medicine or other humanitarian aid for Iraq or Kuwait. Passed September 24 (15-0).

670

Expands embargo to include all air cargo traffic, except U.N.-authorized humanitarian aid; U.N.-member nations asked to detain Iraqi ships that may be used to break the naval embargo. Passed September 25 (14-1), with Cuba opposing.

674

Holds Iraq liable for war damages and economic losses; asks for evidence of human rights abuses by occupying forces; demands embassies in Kuwait be restocked with food and water and demands release of hostages. Passed October 29 (13-0), with Cuba and Yemen abstaining.

677

Condemns Iraq's alleged attempts to drive out Kuwaitis and repopulate their country; asks U.N. Secretary General to take possession of Kuwait's census and citizenship records for safekeeping. Passed November 28 (15-0).

678

Gives Baghdad "one final opportunity" until January 15 to comply with resolutions. After that date, nations allied with Kuwait are authorized "to use all necessary means" to force Iraq to withdraw and honor the resolutions. Passed November 29 (12-2), with China abstaining and Cuba and Yemen opposing.

Associated Press   Source: *Minneapolis Star Tribune* newspaper, March 1, 1991

Index